Morley Roberts

The Western Avernus

Toil And Travel in Further North America

Morley Roberts

The Western Avernus
Toil And Travel in Further North America

ISBN/EAN: 9783744759663

Printed in Europe, USA, Canada, Australia, Japan

Cover: Foto ©Andreas Hilbeck / pixelio.de

More available books at **www.hansebooks.com**

THE WESTERN AVERNUS

OR

TOIL AND TRAVEL

IN

FURTHER NORTH AMERICA

BY

MORLEY ROBERTS

LONDON
SMITH, ELDER, & CO., 15 WATERLOO PLACE
1887

TO MY FRIENDS

THE AUTHORS OF 'THYRZA' AND 'THE CRYSTAL AGE'

CONTENTS.

CHAPTER		PAGE
I.	IN TEXAS	1
II.	BULL-PUNCHING	18
III.	IOWA AND MINNESOTA	26
IV.	IN ST. PAUL	37
V.	TO MANITOBA AND THE ROCKIES	52
VI.	THE KICKING HORSE PASS	63
VII.	THE RAILROAD CAMPS	74
VIII.	THE COLUMBIA CROSSING	95
IX.	THE TRAIL ACROSS THE SELKIRKS	103
X.	THE GOLDEN RANGE AND THE SHUSHWAP LAKES	125
XI.	ROUND KAMLOOPS	139
XII.	THROUGH THE FRASER CAÑON	153
XIII.	DOWN STREAM TO THE COAST	171
XIV.	NEW WESTMINSTER	179
XV.	BACK TRACKS TO EAGLE PASS	200
XVI.	TO VANCOUVER ISLAND AND VICTORIA	225
XVII.	MOUNT TACOMA OVERHEAD	232
XVIII.	OREGON UNDERFOOT	247
XIX.	ACROSS THE COAST RANGE	260
XX.	IN SAN FRANCISCO	283

THE WESTERN AVERNUS.

CHAPTER I.

IN TEXAS.

THE wide prairie of North-west Texas, with Nature's sweet breath bearing faint odours of spring flowers, was around me; a plain of few scant trees or smaller brush, with here and there a rounded hill that emphasised the breadth of level land, and again the general surface broken, by quiet creeks and winter rain, into hollow cañons beneath me, and beyond them once more the gentle roll of grassy prairie, and hills again. I looked around me and I was alone; and yet not wholly solitary, for about me strayed a band of sheep, grazing the sweet grasses that were so green when near, and which showed a faint tinge of purple or delicate blue afar off. I was a Texas sheepherder. A month before I had walked the crowded desolation of unnatural London.

My life had been one of many changes. From

the North of England to the wide brown plains of sunburnt Australia; from her again to the furrows of the ocean for many months of seaman's toil and danger; then England's greatest city and life, irksome and delightful by turns in her maze and prison; then ill-health, with all its melancholy train, and sudden feverish resolution to shake from myself the chains I began to loathe.

And it was thus I came to Texas, the land of revolution and rude romance, and pistol arbitration, whither my brother had long preceded me—a land of horses, cattle, and sheep, of cotton and corn, a land of refuge for many crimes, and for those tired and weary even as I was. So outward civilisation was gone, and it was with strange feelings of delight that I came into a new country to commence a new career, although I knew that there would inevitably be much labour and perhaps much suffering for me.

I came into a Texas town by no means greatly different from other American towns that I had seen and passed through in my swift flight south and west from the Atlantic seaboard, save that all around it was open unfenced prairie, with no fertile farms or houses to indicate that a town was near at hand. But I found, to my surprise, that Colorado City was cold on that spring morning of 1884, and I was unprepared for it, for I thought myself far enough south to demand as my right perpetual warmth and sunshine; and it was only when I learnt that I stood on a plateau two thousand feet above the sea level that the cold did not seem unnatural. My impressions of the town and its people were favourable. There were many men walking round the streets dressed in wide-brimmed hats, leather leggings with fringe adornments, long boots, with large spurs rattling as they went. They were mostly tall and strong, and I noticed with interest the look of calm assurance about many of them, as if they had said to themselves : ' I am a man, distinctly a man, nobody dares insult me ; if anyone does, there will be a funeral—and not mine.'

Then the ordinary citizens of the place seemed ordinary citizens, in nowise remarkable, and, as far as I could see, neither they nor the others, who were, as I soon discovered, the much-talked-of cow-boys, wore knives or revolvers.

In fact, my impressions were exactly what they should not have been, according to Bret Harte. From him I had taken my notions of Western America, and I had constructed an ideal in the air, in which red-shirted miners, pistolling cow-boys, reckless stage-drivers, gentlemanly gamblers, and self-sacrificing women figured in a kind of kaleidoscopic harlequinade, ending up in a snow-storm or the smoke of a gunpowder massacre. And I was disappointed ; but I must not be unjust to a favourite author of mine, for I owed it to my own imagination.

My brother was living in this town, and it was with very little difficulty that I discovered him. We shook hands and sat down, running through our different experiences. I detailed my disgust of London and the life I had led there. He gave discouraging accounts of Texas, averring that the water was vile, that 'fever and ague' was common, that it was too hot in summer and too cold in winter. I learnt from him that almost everybody in town carried revolvers concealed under his coat-tails or inside his waistcoat, and that people were occasionally shot in spite of the peaceful look of the place. Nevertheless, there was little danger for a man who was in the habit of minding his own business, who was not a drinker and quarrelsome, and did not frequent gambling-houses and saloons. I vowed I would go into none of them, and promptly broke it when I went down town with my brother to get clothes such as Texans wear, for he himself took me into one and introduced me to a gentlemanly gambler, who might have stepped bodily out of the story of 'Poker Flat'—a Georgian, dark and slim, with long hair, dressed in black, amiable looking, and a quiet desperado if need were.

I changed my apparel under Jack's advice and appeared in the streets in a very wide-brimmed grey felt hat and long boots reaching to my knees, and then, when I was 'civilised,' as he declared, we went to his boarding-house, and he introduced me to a circle of Texan working men. I made myself at home, and sat quietly listening to the talk about the war—a subject the Southerner is never weary of—of desperadoes, of cattle, and of sheep. Jack and I held a council of two as to what was to be done. I wanted to work on a sheep or cattle ranche, as I had learnt the ways of these in Australia, and, although he had not ever followed that business himself, he agreed to go with me if we could obtain such work. A few days afterwards we left the city in the waggon of a sheep-owner, hired to do the work of herders for 25 dols., or about 5*l.*, a month.

So I once more dwelt under canvas, living a pastoral life, cooking rude meals in the open air on the open prairies, forty long miles to the northward of the town. And we went to work, building sheep 'corrals' or pens of heaped, thorny mesquite brush, bringing in firewood, cutting it, putting up tents—for my part glad to be so far from men in that sweet fresh air, for I began to feel alive, volitional, not dead and most basely mechanical as at home in England.

We were in camp on the border of the creek that ran by us with sluggish flow, as if it lacked the energy to go straight forward. In front of us, to the south, was a semicircle of bluffs, up which one had to climb to gain the open prairie, that stretched out green and grey as far as eye could reach. Beneath the bluffs was a level with thin mesquite trees, and on the banks of the creek a few cotton woods, and beyond it another level with thicker brush, and then a mass of broken, watercut land, formed into small fantastic cañons that bit deep into the red earth, and clay, and gravel, that lay beneath.

I led a busy life—up before sunrise, in after sundown. Then we sat round the camp-fire, smoking and talking. Our boss was an Englishman, one Jones, fair and pleasant; with him another fatter, ruddier Englishman, young, bumptious, and green withal, but no bad companion. Beside them a Mexican, long-haired, with glittering dark eyes under the shade of his big sombrero, small and active, taciturn for want of English. I could have warranted him a talker had we known his own sweet tongue. But my Spanish was limited to a few oaths—Caramba!—with some others terrible to be translated, and Don Quixote in the original has yet to be mastered. Then another herder, myself, and Jack. Decidedly, England was in the ascendant, and our Spaniard looked on dumbly, in contemplation, as his lithe fingers rolled cigarettes one after another in the yellow Mexican paper, dipping into his little linen bag for the dry tobacco.

At daylight breakfast, after a wash in the creek. Bacon and bread and coffee, morning, noon, and night, with rare mutton and beans, red and white, cooked with grease and greasy. Then I went to the corrals and let out my sheep and their lambs, the oldest skipping merrily and the little new-born ones weakly tottering and baaing piteously, while the anxious mothers watched their offspring, turning round to lick them, looking at me suspiciously the while.

With them I spent day after day on the prairie in almost utter solitude, save for the gentle animals I held in charge. These would scatter out and fleck the green prairie with white of wool, browsing on brush and sweet grass, while the lambs played round them, taking tentative doubtful bites at the grass, as if not yet assured that anything but milk was good for them, or stood sucking or lay asleep ; sometimes waking suddenly with a loud baa of surprise to find themselves in such a strange wide world, and then rushing motherwards for milk, butting with persistence the patient ewes, who moved along gently after other uncropped grasses. And at ten o'clock, when the sun grew fierce, they would take their noon-time's siesta, lying down under the scant shade of mesquites or the few rocks at the end of the bluffs that ran down to the creek. They slept and woke, got up one at a time, walking round, then down again. And I picked a shady tree myself, taking all the shade, not through selfishness, but they yielded it to me for fear. I ate my little lunch, and drank water from the round tin flask encased in canvas that I bore over my shoulder, and smoked a peaceful pipe, and read a book I had brought out with me, or dreamed of things that had been, and of things not yet to be. And birds came round, perching on the woolly backs of sheep—birds of blue and birds of red, some with sweet songs. And from the shelter of low thick brush or tufts of heavier grass peeped a silvery skinned snake with beady eyes, drawing back on seeing me. Or a little soft-furred cotton-tail rabbit whisked from one bush to another, throwing up his tuft of a tail and showing the white patch of under fur that gives him his name, gleaming like cotton from the bursting pod. And that yonder? It was a jack rabbit, a hare, long-legged, quick running; but then he went slowly, and sat up and looked at me as if he were a prairie dog of yonder town of quaint, brown, sleek-furred marmots, whose cry is like that of chattering angry birds. But he swerved aside suddenly, Mr. Jack Rabbit. The sheep would not frighten him, and I was as quiet as the windless tree I sat under. It was a snake, not silver, but brown and diamonded. He saw me coming and slipped under the rock, and lay there, making a strange noise, new to me but unmistakable. He was a rattlesnake. Then maybe I would go a little way from my herd and see an antelope on the distant prairie, and between me and the deer, a sly, slinking coyoté, swift-footed and cunning, a howler at nights, making a whole chorus by himself; by quick change of key persuading the awakened shepherd that there was a band of them on the bluff in the moonlight looking down hungrily on the corralled and guarded sheep.

Day by day this pastoral life went on, not all as

sweet as an idyll, but with some content. But my brother fell ill, and went back to town, and I was left to my own experience, which grew by contact with my Texan neighbours, with whom I got along pleasantly, as I was fast relapsing into primitive barbarism. I read little, and the noon I spent in contemplation, or observation of the denizens of the prairie, and at night the hour before sleep was spent in smoking and chatter, and grumbling at the sameness of the cookery.

I herded through all April, but in the beginning of May I began to grow very weary of the work, and begged Jones to give me something else to do, no matter what, so that I was not compelled to act dog to his sheep any more. I was evidently unfit for a herder, for the task grew harder instead of easier. At last my 'boss' went into town and brought out another man, and released me. I went to corral-building, and wood-chopping, and to preparations for shearing, which would soon be; and as I then had Sunday free, I used to go fishing for cat-fish in the creek, and caught more often demoniacal mud turtles, which I unhooked with much fear of their snappish jaws. And one Sunday I slew a great rattlesnake nearly five feet long, as thick as my fore-arm. At the end of his tail, as he lay half coiled up, was a cloud—strange, undiscernible—the loud rattles in fierce, quick vibration. I went into a state of instinctive animal fury, and killed him with a branch wrenched from a mesquite, regardless of the sharp thorns that made my hands bleed.

Our days and nights now grew warmer with advancing summer, which passed across the prairie and left it barer and brown, and doubtless made the dull sheep remember, if remember they can, past shearings of other years' fleeces and quick coolness. And shearing-time came on apace, for there were no more sudden 'northers' that came from the frozen north, that knows no early spring, to make us shiver in our sleep and wake in early morning cursing the climate.

So, when our preparations were complete, the wool-table set up in the corral, the wool-boxes for tying the soft fleeces ready, the posts and cross-pieces erected, for the canvas shelter to keep the glaring noon sun from the backs and bared necks of the stooping shearers, Jones went round and summoned the 'boys' to start to work. And our camp took a livelier aspect with its Texan youngsters. The English element was in the minority. Then the 'boss' went to town for more shearers, and came back with a band of Mexicans, who looked at the white men sulkily, thinking, no doubt, that there would not be so much money to be made, as they were not to have 'las boregas' to themselves. Among them was an Indian, a dark-skinned Chickasaw, who spoke a little English, and confided to me that he thought very little of the Mexicans. These were finer men, though, than my little wizened Indian—tall, some of them, with easy motion, dark eyes, dark hair, over which the inevitable sombrero of wide shade, with vast complications of plaited adornments around it, making it look heavy and cumbersome.

Next day shearing began. Sheep huddled together in the corral bleating for their lambs, or running to and fro for those left outside. Under the rude festoons and curves of canvas, the wooden platform, with a few sheep in front, and on the board itself seven Mexicans, and the Chickasaw, and four Texan boys bending over the sheep. The sharp click, click of the moving, devouring shears of sharp steel, and the fair fleece, white and pure, falling back over the outer unclean wool yet unshorn. The last cut, and the loosed fleece-bearer, uncloaked and naked, runs shaking itself into the crowding others, wondering 'if it be I,' and another dragged unwillingly by the hind leg from its companions, while the parted fleece goes in a bundle of softness to the table, to be tied and tossed to the man who treads down the wool in the suspended woolsack, for we are primitive here and have no press. The clean new boards underneath us grow black, and every splinter has its lock of wool. There is wool everywhere, and the taste and smell of it; we are greasy with the grease of it, and hurt fingers smart with it, some little revenge for the pain the sheep have for careless cuts, that run red blood on the divided fleece.

And night time came, and the sheep stood in the

corral hungry, and wishing the vile yearly business was over. And when we got up next morning there was not a Mexican to be seen. They had disappeared in the night, doubtless angry that there were white men to divide the profits with them. Jones 'cavorted' round somewhat, abusing Mexicans generally, swore he would have no more to do with them, and went for more white men. I sheared among these in order to learn this noble pastoral art, as I wished to learn everything else, for no man knows when his knowledge may be useful and even necessary to him. So we had none of 'los Mexicanos,' with their fearful oaths, among us, and no Chickasaws or Choctaws. And for two days the shearing went well; then came a cold day, congealing the grease in the wool until it clogged the shears. One man, the boaster of the crowd, left, as *he* said, because the sheep were too hard to shear; as *we* said, because he was irritated that a boy sheared eighty while he got through no more than fifty. Then, as Jones was away, my fat ruddy young countryman had charge, and, being unaccustomed to authority and lacking tact, quarrelled with one, which led to all the rest leaving. So the patient sheep were not yet shorn. Jones came back to find things at a standstill, and, being a good-tempered man, only swore a little at white men. But the shearing had to be done, and the vow about Mexicans had to be recanted. The waggon went into town, and in two days eleven more Mexicans came out, better men and better shearers than our first band. The captain—*el capitan*—was a broad-shouldered, lithe-waisted man, quick, keen, black, and comely; with him a one-armed shearer, a great surprise to me, whose first movements on the board I watched with interest. He and the captain sheared in company, and between them made more money than any other two—made it shearing and gambling as well, for the maimed man was an adept at the cards, handling them with a rapidity and dexterity many of his two-handed companions envied and suffered from. I still sheared with them, but not regularly, for sometimes I tied wool, and sometimes pressed it, and even occasionally herded again. I found them friendly, and at night they sang melancholy Mexican love-songs or gambled with the light of a solitary candle, crowding together in one small tent, while I sat amongst them, rolling up cigarettes, as they did, catching a few words of their talk; or I left them and sat by the fire with Jones and the other herders, and perhaps a stray cow-boy who came to sleep at our camp, or some of the young sons of our near neighbours; and in their conversation I got the relish of a new dish that tickled my civilised palate strangely. The flash of humour, the ready rough repartee that permitted no answer, tumbling one to the ground like a sudden tightening lasso dropped over head and shoulders, were like singlestick play after rapier and dagger, hard but harmless.

And at last shearing was over, and my Mexican friends took their money, doubtless resolving to get drunk and gamble in town, and make up for the labour through which they had gone ; and I began to think of going too, for I had heard from my brother in far northern Minnesota, and he asked me to come if it were possible. I was ready enough to go, for it did not seem to me that I was as well as I should be. Perhaps the alkali water was doing me no good, and I should feel better doubtless in the more bracing northern air, drinking the purer streams that ran from Minnesota's lakes and sweet-scented pine woods. I would leave Texas behind me, and the open prairie and its sheep, and bands of long-horned cattle, its chattering prairie dogs and howling coyotés, and prowling cougars, and try another country.

But before I could get away there were many things to do, and some things to suffer—notably a storm one night, a surprise to me, for it seemed that the wind blew calmly on the high plateau, using its energy in ceaseless breezes, not in sudden destructive cyclonic convulsion. But one day the breeze failed. The clouds came up from all quarters, opening and shutting, closing in the blue, dark and thunderous, with pallid leaden edges. We sat in our camp, not thinking greatly about the matter, for so many threatened storms had blown over. But presently Jones got up, and went across the creek to the house, remarking that he thought we should have rain. The young Englishman soon followed, leaving me with Alexander, an American herder, and Bill, a Missourian.

Presently we heard thunder, and a few heavy drops of rain fell. We left the fire, and went into the big tent and sat down. Then there was a low roar of wind, and the rush of rain came with the wind and struck the tent, that bellied in and strained like a sail at sea. One moment of suspense, and, before we could move, the tent was flat on top of us, and the howl of the gale and the pattering of rain were so tremendous that we could not hear ourselves shouting. One by one we crawled out, and in a moment were drenched to the skin. Our oilskins were under the tent; it was utterly impossible to get them. The force of the wind was so great that I could not stand upright, and the rain, coming level on it, blinded me if I tried to look to windward. The lightning, too, was fearful, and the thunder seemed right over and round me. In the dark I got separated from my companions, and crawled on my hands and knees to a small mesquite and held on to it, while every blast bent it down right over me After a while I grew tired of staying there, and in a little lull I made a bolt for the end of the corral, which was a stone wall. Here I got some shelter, though I was afraid that the whole wall might blow over on me. As it was, some of the top stones were dislodged. So I stood up and leaned on it, with my face towards the wind and my broad-brimmed hat over my eyes to keep the sharp sting of the rain off. In front of me were the sheep, and leaning over the wall I could touch them; yet such was the darkness that I could see nothing till the lightning came, and then they stood out before me a mass of white wool, with the lightning glistening on their eyeballs for a momentary space. Then darkness. In one flash I could see Alexander under one mesquite, and, twenty yards from him, Bill under another. I shouted to them, but the wind carried my voice away. Here I stayed for two hours. Then the wind began to lull and the lightning to grow more distant; so, plucking up courage, and waiting for lightning to give me my direction, I walked over to Alexander, and then all three got together again. I wanted them to come over to the house, for we could go round by the road without crossing the creek, which here ran in a horseshoe. Alexander said he would come, for he did not want to be wet all night without any sleep, but we could not persuade Bill. No, he wasn't going to get lost on the prairie such a night as that; he knew where he was, and that was something. So we left him. It took us more than an hour to go less than a mile, for it was still blowing and raining hard, and the lightning was even yet vivid enough to blind us. Once we got off the road, but I managed to find it again, and about one o'clock we came to the house, where Jones and Harris laughed at the wretched figures we cut. However, we got out blankets, and, throwing off our wet clothes, we soon forgot the storm. Next morning the creek was full to its banks, and still rising. We found Bill at the camp, still wet through, though he had managed to find some dry matches and light a fire. Both tents were down. The provisions in the smaller one were all wet and much damage done. Still it was well nothing worse happened. I do not think I shall ever forget that night in Texas.

Three days afterwards, when Jones began to haul his wool to town, I went in with him and Colonel Taylor, his next neighbour, who was hauling for him. It took a day and a half to get to Colorado, and during the first day I killed seven rattlesnakes and two others.

On getting near to town we began to see signs of the damage done by the storm. We were on the banks of the Lone Wolf Creek, that runs into the Colorado River. The waters had run out on the prairie on both sides and swept the grass flat. Against every tree was a bunch of drifted bush and grasses, while here and there I saw a poor little prairie owl or prairie dog, or a snake, strangled by the water or struck by blown branches. In town, houses had been washed away bodily, going down the creek, and others had been turned round on the wooden blocks beneath them. The whole place wore a dishevelled, disarranged look, as if some mischievous giant had been through it, making sport for himself. It was the severest gale ever known in North-west Texas.

C

CHAPTER II.

BULL-PUNCHING.

I WAS in Colorado City again, with resources only forty-five dollars, or about nine pounds English, and had to go north to Minnesota, find my brother and support myself, until I found employment again, on that small sum. It was quite evident that I should be unable to pay my fare to St. Paul, Minnesota, and I had to decide now what was to be done. Problem : twelve or thirteen hundred miles to be overpassed without paying one's fare over the rails. This would have been an easy task to many, and some months later it would have scarcely caused me so much anxious thought, but I was then inexperienced and somewhat green in the matter of passes, which are often to be obtained by a plausible man of good address, and in the methods of 'beating the road,' or, more literally, cheating the company.

My brother had told me that it was frequently possible to go long distances with men who had charge of cattle for the great meat markets of St. Louis and Chicago, and had, with an eye to the future, introduced me to a rough-looking young fellow who was an Englishman, but whose greatest pleasure consisted in being mistaken for a native Texan. He followed the profession of a 'bull-puncher,' that is, he went in charge of the cattle destined for slaughter and canning in the distant North, and made money at it, being steady and trustworthy and no drinker.

Jones and I had come to town on Saturday, and on Sunday morning I went to the stockyards to look about me, to watch them putting the cattle in the cars, and to see if I might find my friend. I found him too quickly, for no sooner did I come to the yard than I met him. He asked me if I wanted to go to Chicago, and offered to take me at once, as the train was ready to 'pull out.' I was in a dilemma. My clothes and blankets were at the boarding-house, my money was in the bank. I told him, and he settled it quickly.

'Leave word for my brother Fred to bring along your things; I will cash your order on the bank.'

I went with him to the office, signed my name on the drover's pass after his, and in five minutes was running at twenty miles an hour over the wide prairie, leaving Colorado City behind the sand dunes in the hollow by the river that gives it a name.

We had seven cars of cattle to look after. The poor wretches had a weary journey before them, and their release would be a sudden death. It was a cruel change from the grassy plains with a limitless extent of sweet grass, to be shut in cars and jolted for more than a thousand miles with but short intervals of rest and release, for they remain in the cars twenty-four hours at a time.

I found this bull-punching a very wearisome and dangerous business. It is too frequently the custom with cattle men to crowd the poor beasts, and put perhaps twenty-two where there is only comfortable room for eighteen or twenty. When a steer lies down he often gets rolled over, and is stretched out flat without power to move, as the others stand upon him. It is the duty of the 'bull-puncher' to see that this does not occur, or to make him get up. For this purpose he carries a pole, ten or twelve feet long, usually of hickory, and in the end of this a nail is driven, the head of which is filed off in order to get a sharp point of half or three-quarters of an inch long, which is used for 'jobbing' the unfortunate animal to rouse him to exert himself, and to make those who are standing on him crowd themselves together to give their comrade a chance. If this point does not effect the desired object, the 'twisters' are used. These are small tacks driven into the pole at and round the end, but not on the flat top, where the sharp point is. By means of these tacks the pole catches in the hair of the steer's tail, and it can be twisted to any desired extent. This method is effectual but very cruel, for I have seen the tail twisted until it was broken and limp; but, as a general rule, as soon as the twisting begins the steer gives a bellow and makes a gigantic effort to rise, which, if the other animals can be kept away, is mostly successful. If other means fail the train is run alongside the first cattle-yards, the car emptied, the steer then having no trouble in getting up, unless seriously injured. But I have found them with nearly all their ribs broken on the upper side, and occasionally they die in the car. If the man in charge is conscientious, he will be all over the train whenever it stops, day or night, but very frequently he sleeps all night and pays no attention to them. The man I was with did most of the work at night, leaving me the day. If he needed help he called, and I served him the same in the day. He was perfectly reckless in what he did, and would do what many will not attempt. He would foolishly risk his life by entering the cars if he found it impossible to make a bullock rouse himself, and as I stood outside holding the lantern for him I was sick with apprehension, seeing him hanging to the iron rails above the sharp long horns that might have run him through like a bayonet. Their eyes glittered in the light I held, and they bellowed with fear and anger. Had he fallen, the chances were a thousand to one against his life; he would have been crushed to death between them or trodden out of the shape of humanity under their hoofs. Sometimes he succeeded, but sometimes all this danger was encountered in vain, and the steer he tried to save would be dead at last.

It was dangerous work clambering round the cars and walking over them when the train was in motion. Dangerous enough at any time, but in the night, when I carried a long pole and a lantern with me, I often thought I should come to a sudden end beneath the wheels. I had to jump on the train, too, when in motion, or be left behind, and at junctions such as Denison to walk among shunting cars and trains and loose engines, whose strong head-lights blinded me, hindering sight of some dark, stealthy, unlighted cars running silently on the next rails.

We fed the cattle at Fort Worth, a bustling busy town, the western capital of Texas, the scene of great railroad riots since then, and at Muskogee, a quiet dull place in the Indian Territory, reserved for Indians—Chickasaws, Choctaws, Cherokees, and others, with less familiar names. I saw but few of these, and the men who loafed and idled round the stations through which we passed on the Missouri, Kansas, and Texas Railroad were for the most part whites, armed with six-shooters, for it is not forbidden to carry them. It seemed strange to see little boys, eleven or twelve years old, strutting round with revolvers hung in their belts. Little desperadoes in training, I thought.

This country was sweet and green, and very pleasant, with great stretches of wood and then open pastures, and good streams and pools of bright water.

We ran through the Territory, through part of Kansas and into Missouri, staying a few hours in Sedalia.

I began now to weary of this endless journey, to weary of the prairie that would never cease, and to long for busy Chicago and well-farmed Illinois. It was time, indeed, for me to reach somewhere, for I had never taken off my clothes since leaving Colorado City, and I slept in snatches, rarely slumbering more than three hours at a time.

We crossed the rapid Missouri at Franklin, and came to Hannibal, on the famous Mississippi. We stayed some hours outside the town to feed the cattle, and then ran through a tunnel hewn out of solid rock on to the long slender bridge across the mighty river. I sat on the top of the cars, watching the immense flood of waters that had come from Montana and had yet to go through many a State to New Orleans and the Gulf of Mexico. Here and there were beautiful islands with plentiful trees, green and peaceful, separated from the busier banks on either hand. The town was almost hidden behind the hill under which we had come, and only its smoke, curling overhead, pointed out the spot of many habitations; and some way down stream on the right was an old picturesque building, that I fancifully converted into an ancient ruined castle, aided by the thin haze and hill shadows. It gave the touch of golden romance and age that one so misses in that new land.

We ran through Illinois and came to the great city of Chicago early on Sunday morning, and we gave up charge of the cattle, which would be almost instantly slaughtered. Then I had to make up my mind as to what I was to do. I went to the post office and found no letters from my brother, although I had asked him to give me directions there how to find him. Perhaps he had written to Colorado City, and I had just missed his letter; perhaps he had left St. Paul, and had missed mine. I was in a dilemma. I knew not whether to go to Minnesota or not. I asked my friend, and he advised me to return to Texas, promising to obtain me work with cattle there, and 'at any rate,' said he, 'you can come up with me again when you want to.' This determined me, and I returned to Colorado City once more.

I spent an idle, careless, novel-reading time for some weeks, for I could find no one prepared to give me cattle to take North, as trade was slack and prices low. I got a note from my brother at last, saying he was near St. Paul still, and would wait for me. But I could not get away again now, and perforce went to amusing myself, making acquaintances in town, mostly people my brother had known. I read and smoked, and went into the gambling saloons, though, fortunately, I have no taste for gambling. Then I met one of my Mexican friends, and he shook hands with me warmly, explaining in broken English that all the others were in the 'calabosa,' or jail, for being drunk and disorderly. And soon afterwards I met them going to work on the road in charge of a warder armed with a long six-shooter. They shouted to me and waved their hands, looking not unhappy, and doubtless thinking it was destiny, and not to be made matter of too much thought. I waved my hat to them and saw them no more.

At last I determined to leave the town. I was sick of it, and not well besides, for the water affected me very injuriously. I began to make energetic inquiries, and at last found a man who took me with him. It was time for me to get away; my money was fairly exhausted, and I did not want to go to work in Texas any more. I left town on July 7 and arrived in Chicago on the 16th; and but one thing of all the journey remains in my mind, and that is the figure of Ray Kern, who had once been a cow-boy in Texas, but was leaving it on account of ill-health, who was to be a companion to me afterwards in some of my other trials and journeys yet to come.

When I bade farewell to my friends, Ray among them, I had but 5 dollars left, or £1 English.

CHAPTER III.

IOWA AND MINNESOTA.

I WONDER if it be possible of one who has never been away from his own country and his friends, who has always been in comfort and reasonable prosperity, to imagine my feelings when I suddenly found myself alone and almost penniless in Chicago? I think it impossible. My desolation was in a way unbounded, for every person I saw of the thousands in that great city, wherein I knew not a soul, save those I had left never to see again, made me feel even more and more lonely. I walked the crowded streets for hours, hardly knowing in what direction I was going nor in what direction I should go. My thoughts turned first towards my brother, who was, in the state of my finances, impossibly far away, and from him to my friends at home. To these I was now a shadow, for they were busy, and one from the many of a life circle is but little. To me they were the only realities, and I was walking among shadows who were nothing, and could be nothing, to me, whose habits and thoughts and modes of life had become, after four years in London, intensely, even morbidly subjective. I had lived those years in a state of intellectual progress, which had culminated in a form of pessimism which only permitted me to see beauty in art—in pictures of Turner, in music of Beethoven, in the poetry of the modern ; and now I was thrown on the sharpest rocks of realism, and the awakening was strange and bitter.

On the second day in the city I was even more melancholy, and it was an almost impossible task for me to seek work. But the necessity of so doing became more and more urgent as my resources became less and less, and I made some efforts to obtain employment on the schooners of Lake Michigan. For I had in the days of my more careless boyhood made a voyage at sea, and along with the memory of storm and calm, of channel and open ocean, remained some of the rough practical knowledge of a sailor's work. But I had lost the calm buoyant confidence and energy of those days, and with the decay of health had come a degree of diffidence which then made it difficult for me to push myself among a crowd of rude and ignorant men, even though I had enough plasticity of outward character to make me, to their careless glance, one of their own class. And the dulness of trade in Chicago that summer added to my troubles, and made me unsuccessful.

That night I thought I should try to save money by sleeping somewhere without paying for a lodging. I had heard in London of boys and men sleeping in

Covent Garden Market, and under the arches of the bridges. And now I was about to add this to my own experiences. I had been told that in the large cities of America it was very commonly the custom for the homeless to sleep in 'box-cars,' which I believe would be called 'goods trucks' in England, and I found at last, late in the evening, a spot where many were standing on the rails in a dark corner not far from Randolph Street. After some little search I discovered an open one, and after entering it and closing the sliding door, I lay down on the bare wooden floor, and with my head on my arms fell asleep. I must have slept about two hours when I was awakened by finding my habitation in motion. I was very little concerned as to where it was going, as I was in no place likely to be worse off than in Chicago, and I might very easily have been better. I left the matter in the hands of destiny, and turning over fell asleep again. But I was again awakened in a few minutes by the car stopping, apparently in some building from the difference of sound. The door was opened, and a man entering the car saw me and said, 'Hallo, partner, have you had a good sleep?' 'Pretty fair,' I said, 'but I guess it's over now.' And I got up to go. The intruder was a kind-hearted fellow, however, and as I went out he told me there were plenty of cars outside that would not be disturbed that night, and directed me where to find them. I thanked him, but soon found myself regarded suspiciously by a man who was the night watchman, who finally ordered me to get out of the yard, which I was obliged to do, as under the circumstances I had no alternative, although I confess to feeling very much inclined to resent his doing his duty. So I went out into the streets once more. It was now after midnight, and I had little desire to walk about all night. So after all my trouble I had a night's lodging, for which I paid 25 cents, and was accommodated in a room villanous enough looking to be the scene of one of Poe's midnight murder tales.

Next morning I was still despondent, and walked about aimlessly enough until I came to the Chicago, Milwaukee, and St. Paul Railroad station. I went in and sat down to rest and to think. My thinking discovered me no hope, but my prolonged stay there was the cause of my again meeting with my travelling companion, Ray Kern. He came in looking miserable enough and pale and ill, but when he saw me he brightened up as I had done, and we, who were but of a day or two's acquaintance, grasped each other's hands as if we had been brothers. Poor Ray was in the same condition as myself, though he had a dollar or two more to balance his being worse in health than I was. We had a long talk of ways and means and aims, and his experience helped us out of Chicago. In all American cities there are employment offices, which, on payment of a fee, furnish work, if any is to be obtained, to suitable applicants. They frequently send labourers long distances on the cars for very trifling sums to work for the railroads, who furnish passes for the number they need. Ray and I went across the road to one of these offices, and found that men were wanted to go to a little town near Bancroft, in North-west Iowa, Kosciusko County, to work on the railroad. The fee required by the office was 2 dols., but all I had now was 1 dol. 50 cents, and I was rather hopeless of getting away, when Ray offered the manager 3 dols. 25 cents to send us both out. After some chaffering this was agreed to, and we were furnished with office tickets, which would be changed at the station for passes. I was now without any money at all—not even a cent. But Ray, whose kindness to me I shall never forget, helped me through the day, and in the evening we started with about twenty others for our destination, 600 miles away. This system of sending labourers to distant points on free passes is naturally taken advantage of by persons who wish to go in the direction of the place where the help is needed or beyond it, and very frequently it happens that on reaching the end of the journey there is scarcely one left of those who started. And it was so in this instance. Of the twenty who left Chicago, Ray and I were the only ones who got out at Bancroft, for the others had quietly disappeared at various stations on the way. We had been about thirty-six hours on the journey, and during this time we had passed through a farming country, which was for the most part uninteresting, and, in the northern part of Iowa, to my eye positively ugly, as it there consisted of level plains with no colour or trees to relieve their dead monotony, save an occasional grove of planted trees near a farm, placed to the north of the buildings to make some shelter from the howling 'blizzards,' or winter storms, that rage for days on the bleak and open prairie. And the natural melancholy of the scene was magnified for me by the hunger, which increased as we travelled, for we were both without money save a solitary half-dollar, which Ray was preserving for emergencies.

When we at last reached our objective point we were not encouraged by what we saw. On a side track, a little way from town, stood three cars, one fitted up as an eating-room with rough tables and benches, and the others as sleeping-rooms with bunks in them. We put our blankets down and went in to get dinner, which consisted of huge chunks of tough, badly cooked beef with bread, and potatoes boiled in their skins. The plates were tin, the cups of the same material, the knives rusty and dirty and blunt. Our companions were of all nationalities, they ate like hogs, and their combined odour was distinctly simian. It was with difficulty Ray and I ate our dinners, hungry as we were, for one had to be energetic to obtain anything at all, and the noise and smell and close quarters made both of us, who were by no means in rude health, feel sick and miserable.

After dinner, if I can call it such, we went out and walked in silence up the line. Presently I burst out, in unconscious imitation of the famous Edinburgh Reviewer, 'This will never do.'

Ray looked up and said shortly, 'Charlie, I agree with you.'

We continued walking, and presently came to a little 'section house.' These are built at intervals along all the lines in America. In them live a 'section boss' and a small gang of men, who look after a certain section of the line, seeing that it is kept in repair. They raise the 'ties' or sleepers if they settle down, renew them when they rot, see that the joints are perfect and the rails in line. Outside the house we met the 'section boss,' who asked us if we had come up to work with the 'gravel-train gang.' We said yes, we had come there with that intention, but didn't much like the look of things, and would prefer not doing it if anything else were possible. He seemed to be in no way surprised at that, and said if we cared to come to him we could go to work in the morning, promising us good accommodation and board, the wages being, however, only $1.25 a day—twenty-five cents less than that of the other job. The cost of board, however, was to be somewhat less. We engaged at once with him, and went back for our blankets, paying our last half-dollar for our miserable mid-day meal.

Our 'boss' was named Breeze, and we found him

and his wife very pleasant and intelligent and kind. The others in the gang were Swedes, who could not talk much English, and Ray and I had very little to do with them during the short time we stayed there. For Ray seemed too weak to work, and using the pick and shovel was so new to me that I made twice the labour of it that the others did; and, moreover, my foot got so sore that I found some difficulty in working with any degree of complacency. After three days we determined to leave and go north to St. Paul, if it could be managed. But we had great difficulty in getting any money, as the men on sections are only paid once a month, when the travelling car of the R.R. Paymaster comes round. But we signed orders for Breeze to receive our money, and got seventy-five cents apiece, one dollar and a half in all, which constituted our sole resources. Mrs. Breeze made us up a parcel of food, and I gave her a little volume of Emerson's 'Essays,' which I had brought from England with me. And thus we started north again. Of all the melancholy days' walks I ever had, that was the most doleful. Around us lay a miserable, flat, most dreary prairie; ahead of us stretched the long line of endless rails, fading in the distance to nothing, and overhead the July sun glared piteously on two disheartened tramps, who were most decidedly out of place, wishing themselves anywhere — anywhere out of that world. Had Ray been well and cheerful, I should have been more dispirited than I was, for in his state of health and mind I had to keep him up by cracking jokes and singing songs when I felt more like making lamentations or taking to sulky silence. But he was so weak that we had to rest, and if I had not kept him going we should have been there now. At noon we camped by a waterhole, or small swamp, and ate a little and had a smoke, and, feeling hot and dust-grimed and wayworn, I stripped off and had a bathe, while Ray looked on in silence. By dint of hard and painful walking we reached a farm in the evening. We went up and asked for work. The superintendent was a Swede, a nice enough fellow. He gave us supper, and next morning set me shocking barley after a reaping and binding machine, while Ray went out haymaking. Our wages were to be a dollar a day and board. On the evening of the second day the owner of the farm, a Congressman named Cooke, came home, and, in American parlance, 'fairly made things hum.' In fact, we had to work too hard altogether, considering that we began at sunrise and worked till it was dark. Ray by no means improved in health, and on that evening we agreed to leave the next day and make another stage to St. Paul. I do not think Cooke minded our going much, as he thought we were unaccustomed to hard work. He came in to give us the three dollars each as I was rolling up my blankets, and noticing that I had a book he asked to see it. It was 'Sartor Resartus.'

Turning it over and over, he looked at it and then at me, and finally said, 'Do *you* read it?' I answered by another question, 'Do *you* suppose I carry it just for the sake of carrying it?' 'Well,' said he, 'I am surprised at a man, who can read a book such as this seems to be, tramping in Iowa.' 'So am I, Mr. Cooke,' I replied, and, bidding him good-day, Ray and I marched off, a little better in spirits, as we now had seven dollars and a half between us.

That night we crossed the northern boundary of Iowa and came into Minnesota at Elmore. We had supper at the hotel, and found out that there was a train going to St. Paul soon after midnight. After supper we went out, and finding an empty box-car we lay down to get some sleep. But the cold and mosquitoes combined made it almost impossible. On no other occasion have I ever found mosquitoes so active in such a low temperature.

At midnight Ray got up, and went over to the conductor of the train and made a bargain with him to take us to Kasota (which was as far as he went with the train) for 1 dol. 50 cents each, which was much under the regular fare. This is very commonly done in the States by the conductors, who put the money in their own pockets. Next day we were in Kasota, a very pretty little place with lots of timber; indeed, Southern and Central Minnesota seem generally well wooded. We found there was a freight train leaving this town at one o'clock, and I went over to find the conductor. I asked him what he would take two of us to St. Paul for. He said, 'Two dollars each.' Now we had by this time only three dollars and three-quarters left, so I told him that wouldn't do, stating how our finances were, and offering him three and a half dollars. After refusing several times, finally he said, 'Very well, you can come along, though I expect you will shake a fifty dollar bill at me when you get to St. Paul.' How devoutly I wished it had been in my power! We jumped into the caboose, and at eleven o'clock that night we arrived in St. Paul. We had then 25 cents between us, which was very encouraging to think of. Five cents of this we gave to the brakeman of our train to show us a car to sleep in. We found one half filled with sawed lumber, crawled into it, spread our blankets, and lay down while our friend held the lantern. His last words were: 'Mind you get out before four o'clock, or you will go down south again.' After about three hours' sleep we were wakened by the yardmen switching or shunting the car, and making up our bundles we dropped them out and followed them when the car next stopped. Near at hand we found a little platform about eight feet square, by a house right in the middle of the railroad yard. On this we spread our blankets, and only woke to find it broad daylight, seven o'clock, and men working all round us. We rolled up again, and in silence went up into the town.

CHAPTER IV.

IN ST. PAUL.

WE placed our blankets and valises in a small restaurant and walked to the post office. I asked four men the way to this building, and of these only the last could speak intelligible English, such are the numbers of Germans and Scandinavians in some parts of the States. I found two post-cards from my brother; one of which stated he was working near the town, giving me an address, and the other, dated two weeks later, gave me to understand that he had been unable to remain in St. Paul owing to scarcity of work, and that he had left the city for New Orleans by the river steamboats. This was not very satisfactory for me, for I had cherished some little hope that he might have been either in a position to help me to work or to repay me some money which I lent him at Ennis Creek. Now I and my partner were truly on our 'beam ends,' and 20 cents alone stood between us and absolute bankruptcy. We walked round the corners from the post office and sat down on a seat in the public park. As consideration, however, was in no way likely to appease our hunger, which was now beginning to be inconveniently perceptible, I left Ray and went to see what could be got for our cash remainder in the shape of breakfast. After tramping awhile I bought a loaf for 10 cents and butter for the rest, and we were now 'dead broke.' Ray was sitting in the same position as I had left him, having no energy to move, poor fellow, and it was with difficulty I got him out of the seat to come and look for a quiet place in which to consume the luxuries with which I was laden. A neighbouring lumber yard seemed suitable, and we found a convenient plank on which I put the paper of salty butter, while I divided the loaf with my knife.

This was a nice meal for two hungry men, but we were glad enough to get it under the circumstances, and since then a loaf would at times have been a very godsend even without the butter. I was sorriest for Ray, for a cup of coffee or tea with his meal would have done him good, and it was as unattainable as champagne or oysters and chablis. When we had finished the bread I wrapped up the remains of the butter and hid it between two planks in a dark corner of the lumber pile, for I thought it possible that we might want it, though there seemed little likelihood of our having bread with it. As we still had tobacco, we lighted our pipes and walked slowly along the street, wondering where the next meal was to come from. Perhaps, if I were placed in the same situation again, I should not, in the light of far bitterer experience, regard it as so dismal, and my increased knowledge and *savoir faire* in things American would show me ways out where I then saw, as it were, 'No thoroughfare' plainly written.

Ray was really too ill to 'rush round,' and he was quite a deadweight on me, for he was hopeless. In ordinary circumstances his knowledge would have helped me, but all it did now was to pessimistically recall the blackest side of his former experience. He thought it almost worse than useless to go to an employment office without money, and so it seemed to me. But when I left him on the park seat, and began to look round without the dear fellow's most dismal croaking to dishearten me, I plucked up courage, after making vain inquiries in various quarters, to try an Employment Agency whose chalked board outside gave evidence of labour needed in many different lines of business. There were fifty men wanted to work on the streets. This I considered was very probable, considering the state they were in. There were more wanted for the waterworks. This, too, would be no work of supererogation. There were teamsters, dairymen, and various others whose services were desired. I walked in and spoke to the manager, who, finding I professed not to be a teamster, though I could drive reasonably well, nor a milkman, for lack of practice, offered me the less lucrative and probably more toilsome job of labourer at the waterworks for the moderate fee of one dollar.

Never had the great American dollar assumed such a gigantic size to me. Never had it seemed so far away. Liberty in her cap was fairly invisible, and the imagined scream of the bold eagle on the reverse was 'faint and far.'

'Well, mister,' said I, 'I have not got a dollar.'

'What have you got?' was his answer, thinking, I suppose, that I might have 99 cents. I surprised him.

'I've got a partner.'

'Has he any money?'

I might have answered in the language of Artemus Ward—'nary cent,' but it did not occur to me.

'He's got as much as I have, and that's nix' (corrupt German for 'nichts').

My friend looked at me, having no further remarks to make. I felt a crisis had come.

'Suppose you send us both out and ask the boss to stop two dollars from our wages on your account. Won't this do? You see we want work; we've got to have it. That's a fact.'

The manager walked to his big desk, wrote a note, sealed it, gave it to me, and said, 'Come here at two o'clock, and you can go out to the works with the provision wagon.' I thanked him very quietly and walked out.

Ray was as I left him. I composed my countenance to sombre dolorousness, and sat down beside him, grunting out 'Got any tobacco?' No, the last was gone. He seemed so miserable that I thought it cruel to deceive him by my looks any longer, and laughed till I woke him fairly up, and he saw by the twinkle in my eyes that I had been in luck. 'So you've got work?' 'Yes,' said I, 'and you too; we go out this afternoon to the waterworks.'

How hard must be one's lot when the news that it is possible to earn a dollar and three-quarters a day, by ten hours of hard manual labour, acts like a very tonic and braces up the whole man! Ray was for the rest of the day quite a new being, in spite of his hunger, which half a small loaf had not gone far to appease in the morning. As for myself, I laughed and joked, and, thinking I should be quite happy if I had some tobacco, I managed to get into conversation with a man near us, borrowed a pipeful, and smoked in calm content.

At two o'clock we found the wagon at the office, put our blankets in it, and set out on our walk, which was seven miles, to the works. After a while, finding the wagon move but slowly and the road plain, we walked on ahead, and when we had made about two-thirds of the way we came on three teamsters who were having dinner. They gave us a friendly hail, and, whether they fancied we looked hungry or not, kindly asked us to sit down with them and 'pile in,' which being interpreted signifies, 'Pitch in and eat.' Under the circumstances such an invitation was by no means to be despised, and accordingly we consumed all there was, yea, even unto the last crust, taking an occasional drink at a very convenient spring, our companions chatting merrily the while and laughing at my semi-tragical, semi-comic account of our adventures since leaving Chicago. These were three good fellows.

After another mile or two's walk we came in sight of the camp, which consisted of two huge tents on the flat and two more on the side of the hill. We could see a great trench or sewer cut in the ground with derricks swinging up large iron buckets of dirt, and men busily employed digging lower down, breaking the ground on the line laid out for excavation, while some were laying beams in the cut to prevent the sides from caving in. So down we went and presented our letter. The boss asked if we had had dinner, and as we said 'No'—thinking it still possible to eat more—he told the cook to give us some, which we had little trouble in getting rid of. And then we went to work with a gang whose boss was called Weed, who was one of the nicest and most kindly men I ever worked under.

However, what he first set me to do very nearly finished me. I had to take a big unwieldy maul, or mallet, and drive down boards into the mud and ooze at one side of the ditch, as they were then cutting through a kind of quicksand. The last week had not made me very much stronger, as may be imagined, and it was only sheer necessity which made me stick to it. But I had to do something, and this was all that seemed to offer itself. Next day was even worse, for I had a big Irishman with me, and as we had to strike one after the other, he made it as hard as he could by working too fast. I had some difficulty in refraining from making a mistake and striking him. However, that evening I made a friend of Weed by offering to splice the rope into the big bucket. This had been done so execrably by another man that, when I turned out a neat and creditable job, he made things as pleasant as he could for me.

We were working with as rough and as mixed a crowd as it has ever been my lot to come in contact with. There were Americans from most of the various States and Territories, there were some Englishmen, and a promiscuous crew of Canadian and European French, Germans, Swedes, Norwegians, Danes, Finns, Polanders, Austrians, Italians, and one or two Mexicans. I didn't see a Turk, but I wouldn't like to say there was none.

We slept in a big tent with about fifty men in it. There were upper and lower bunks, each holding two men. Ray and I secured a top one, and had for our left-hand companions two Swedes, while on our right was an Irishman and an American named Jack Dunn. I do not know what State he was from. This man was feared by everyone in the tent. He was to all appearance exceedingly powerful, and when in a bad temper ferocious and ready to quarrel 'at the drop of a hat,' as the American saying goes. At first he seemed to dislike me, and made some remarks about Englishmen in general which I declined in such company to make any cause for a disturbance. In a day or two, however, he distinguished me by honouring me with his friendship, and we would talk for hours while lying in our bunks, none of the rest caring to object, even if they wanted to sleep.

He had not been two weeks out of jail when I saw him, and he gave me accounts both of how he got in and how he got out. And both showed him to be a desperate man, and most uncommonly courageous.

It appeared he had been firing in a Mississippi steamboat, and while he was in the stokehole one of the negroes came past him with a box and struck him on the elbow. 'I cussed the black——,' said Jack, 'and he answered me back. I never could stand sass from a nigger, and I picked up a lump of coal and threw it at him. He didn't give me any more talk. He died by the time we made the next landing, and you bet I just lighted out in the dark. They were after me, but it was more than a month before they took me. So I got eighteen months' hard labour for manslaughter. I thought of escaping, but couldn't see a chance, and had been there nine months when another chap escaped. I was just mad to think that one man had the grit in him to skip, while I lay in the thundering hole still, but when it came out how he tried, I didn't care for that way. You see his partner four days after told how it was. He had crawled down a drain. The warder got to hear of it, and of course off he goes to the governor. The governor just said, "If he went that way, he's in there yet." For you see there was a grating or bars across the drain 120 feet down it. Down they goes to see it, and sure enough there was a mighty bad smell came out there. 'Twould pretty nigh knock you down. The governor he gets us all out and tells us this: "Now, boys," sez he, "I want No. 20 out of there, and if I break down to him it will take days and days, for it's all solid stone and concrete over where he is; and, besides, it will cost a pile o' money. Now, if there's anybody here with a sentence of less than two years, I'll see that he shall get half of the full term remitted, if he'll go down that pipe and fetch him out."

'Well, we all just looked at each other; some seemed as if they'd speak, some turned red and pale. I thought my heart was a-bursting, I heard it go thump, thump. At first I couldn't speak too, but I thought if another chap speaks afore me I'd just kill him as I did the nigger. I holds up my hand, and when the governor looked at me I says in a kind of queer voice, as seemed to belong to somebody else, "I'll do it, sir." The other chaps looked at me. Mebbe they thought I was as good as dead too. Some looked glad, as if I'd kind o' took the 'sponsibility off 'em. And how did I feel? I guess I felt all right in less than a minute. You see I was tired of the stone walls, and

I seemed to see the river outside, and feel the wind coming right through the solid jail, so I kind of freshened up.

'Well, the boss he dismissed the other men, and him and me and two or three of the warders goes down to the pipe. I can't tell you just what size it was. It was just big enough for me to squeeze into. There was a coil of rope, about as thick as my thumb, and after taking off all my clothes but a flannel shirt and drawers and socks, I coils a yard or two round my shoulders, catches hold in my hand, and got in, with the rope tied round my heels so they could drag me and him out.

'They told me I wasn't in more than twenty minutes. Dunno. Seems to me I served nine months in there; the stink was just terrible, and the further I got in the worse it was. And breathing! Jehoshaphat! I panted like a tired dog, and I thought I would burst. Sometimes I seemed to kind o' swell up, and I couldn't move. And then, dark as it was, I seemed to see fire and sparks, and my eyes were hot, and I thought they was a-dropping out. One time I think I got insensible, but I suppose I kept on crawlin', for the warder that paid out the rope sez I never stopped till I got him. Oh yes, I got him, after crawlin' through all the narrow drains in America, drawing miles of rope that got so heavy and hard to drag that every inch seemed the last I could go.

Christ, I wouldn't do it for the world again! Before I knew it I touched something cold and clammy with my burning hands, and I shrunk up as if I'd touched a jelly-fish swimming in muddy water. I got a hitch over his heels, and they tightened up the rope; as I told 'em to do if I stopped and gave it a pull. And I don't remember anything more till I found myself outside in the air, with something lying near me covered with a tarpaulin. The doctor was bending over me, washing the blood off my face, for draggin' me out insensible I got scratched in the face on the pipe-joints, you see. I lay in the hospital two days, and every time I went to sleep I dreamt I was in there with No. 20. Then they let me out, and I came here. Good-night, partner.'

There was also in the same tent a man named Gunn, a very fine-looking young fellow, from Maine, who had been three years in British Columbia, where, according to his own account, he had earned a great deal of money by making 'ties' or sleepers for the Canadian Pacific Railroad. This he had spent in seeing his friends. And he was now trying to make a 'stake,' or a sum sufficient to take him back there. We had a great deal of conversation about that country, and I was infected with the desire of seeing it. It used to seem to me in England that it was almost the furthest place from anywhere in the world, and this had some effect in forming my plans, as I was too adventurous to remain satisfied in such a well-known, near-at-hand spot as Minnesota.

I stayed at the works twelve days, during which time I worked with the pick and shovel, rigged derricks, spliced ropes, and mixed mortar for the bricklayers, as the water was to run through a brick tunnel instead of iron pipes, where the quicksand was. On one occasion the man I was working with irritated me, and I went over to Weed and asked him to give me my 'time'—*i.e.* to make up what time I had worked there in order that I might get my money. He said, 'Oh, nonsense, what's the matter with you? I think you're a little bad tempered this morning. *I* don't want you to go away, so go back to work.' I went back and stayed four more days, but so anxious was I to get away from such detestable work and companions that I made all the overtime I could. At last I worked one day ten hours in the ditch, went to supper at six, at seven came back, and with a little German for partner, pumped all night till six in the morning, then had breakfast, slept two-and-a-half hours, worked from 9.30 till six in the evening, and after supper again went out pumping till midnight. At a quarter to twelve I lay down on a pile of loose bricks, as we were pumping turn and turn about, and fell asleep. At midnight two others came to relieve us, and it was with difficulty they woke me up.

Next morning I got what money was coming to me and went into town. Ray would not come, so

I shook hands with him, bidding him farewell. I now had a new partner, who was not so much to my mind as Ray, and of entirely different character. Pat M'Cormick was an American Irishman who had lived mostly in Michigan and Wisconsin, working in the pine-woods and 'driving' on the rivers. This driving is taking the logs, which are sledded to the rivers from where they are cut, down into the lakes, and is a hazardous and laborious employment. The drivers are wet for weeks together, and mostly up to their middles in icy water; they stand on the logs going down rapids which would destroy a boat, they ease them over the shoals, and break 'jams' that occur when some logs get caught and those floating behind them are stopped by them. Pat was a great drinker, which unfortunately I did not find out till too late, and besides, utterly reckless, though good tempered to an extreme when sober.

We walked into town, creating some little amusement in the more respectable streets by our appearance. I had still my big-brimmed Texas hat on me, which at the camp had earned me the title of 'Texas,' under which sobriquet I went for many months, as it was passed on from one acquaintance of mine to another. Our boots were long knee-boots, and of course uncleaned, and our blankets looked as if we had just come off the tramp.

We walked round a little, and presently came to an employment office. Outside was a large notice.

CANADIAN PACIFIC RAILROAD.

In British Columbia and the Rocky Mountains.

1,000 Labourers wanted at good wages.
100 Tie-makers wanted by the day, or by the piece.
Steady work guaranteed for two years.

Perhaps, if I had not spoken with Gunn at the camp, I might have passed this by, but his eulogistic account of British Columbia had made me rather anxious to go there. Besides, the natural tendency of everyone seems to be to go west in America. In Australia I had found it impossible to avoid getting farther and farther into the heart of the country, and it is possible that, if I had not made at last a determined effort to get back to Melbourne, I should in time have come out at the Gulf of Carpentaria. Here I had to go west, under the direction of destiny, epitomised in Horace Greeley's 'Go west, young man, and grow up with the country.'

We went in, and found that the fee required was $8\frac{1}{2}$ dols., or about 35s., for which we were to be carried 1,600 miles through Canada to the Rocky Mountains. As M'Cormick had insufficient money, I did for him what Ray Kern had done for me in Chicago—paid the extra amount, and, having bought provisions with the balance of our money, we went off to spend the day as best we could, for we were not to start till the following morning. That night we crossed the river, and finding a pile of hay in front of an unfinished house we crawled into it and slept very well there. Next morning we found ourselves on our way with about one hundred companions, some of whom were in various stages of intoxication, while others were in the deepest dumps consequent to such a state.

CHAPTER V.

TO MANITOBA AND THE ROCKIES.

IT was the morning of August 7 that I left St. Paul. With our last money, as I said, we had bought provisions, which consisted of a couple of loaves, some cheese, and a long sausage, with a few onions and two or three green peppers. After buying this I had twenty-five cents left.

All the 7th was consumed in running north from St. Paul to the Canadian line, which from the Lake of the Woods to the Gulf of Georgia follows the forty-ninth parallel of latitude. After getting clear of the Minnesota forests we ran into the Red River Valley, which to the eye seems a perfectly level plain, green and grassy but absolutely treeless. At nightfall we were at Glyndon, a few miles from the Dakota line and Fargo. At midnight we passed the Dominion line at St. Vincent and were in Manitoba, through the whole extent of which the same character of the country prevails as in Northern Minnesota. We reached Winnipeg that morning, and I devoted an hour to seeing what I could of the town, which seemed to me to be an entirely execrable, flourishing and detestable business town, flat and ugly and new. The climate is said to be two months black flies, two months dust, and the remainder of the year mud and snow. The temperature in winter goes down sometimes to sixty degrees below zero, which the inhabitants will often tell you is not disagreeable; 'if you are well wrapped up, as the Polar bear said when he practised his skating,' I thought.

My partner, M'Cormick, came to me a few minutes before the train started and asked if I had any money.

'What for?' said I.

Pat was ready with his answer. 'If you have, it won't be any good after leaving here, and I want some whisky.'

'Well, Mac, if I give it you, you'll get drunk.'

'Drunk! I never was drunk in my life. Come, Texas, you may as well. What's the good of money if you don't spend it?'

'If I do,' I answered, 'you'll repent it before long, you bet your life; and as to your never being drunk, why you're drunk now.' And so he was, for some of the others had been passing the bottle round freely. But it wasn't any use trying to put him off, so, for the sake of peace and quietness, I let him have the last twenty-five cents I had, and he got a small flask of whisky.

As I refused to drink any he drank most of it

himself, with the result that he began quarrelling with one of a bridge gang who boarded the train at Winnipeg. The altercation would have been amusing if Mac hadn't kept on appealing to me, trying to drag me into his troubles. He called the bridgeman a very opprobrious name, and for a moment there was great danger of a 'rough house' out of hand. Mac wanted him to get off the train when it stopped to have it out, but the other man, though not very peaceable by any means, was not so drunk as my partner, and had sense enough not to get left on the prairie for the sake of a fight. So they sat opposite each other wrangling for hours, while I expected their coming to blows every moment. Presently Mac came over.

'Texas, give me your six-shooter.'

'I haven't got one.'

'Oh yes, you have; I know it's in your blankets. I want it.'

'Well, Mac,' I said, getting a little mad, 'in the blankets or not, you won't get it.'

Mac went off, muttering that I was a pretty partner not to help him. Presently the bridgeman came over and sat down by my side. He began with drunken courtesy:

'Sir, I thank you for not giving him your gun. Perhaps you saved my life.' Then getting ferocious: 'Not that I'm scared of him.' Then a short silence, and glaring fiercely at me: 'Nor of you either. I've seen cow-boys, bigger men than you, and with bigger hats too, but they didn't tire me. No, they didn't tire me any.'

'That's good, pard,' said I; 'don't get tired on my account. I'm a quiet man, and don't often kill anybody.'

He looked at me for a while, muttering, and got up to go, saying, 'Oh no, he can't scare this chicken, bet your life.'

A great many kept taking me for a regular cow-boy who had got out of his latitude, especially as Mac would always call me Texas. And to illustrate the absurd ideas so prevalent about the cow-boy, I may mention that when we were about to approach Moose Jaw, in the North-West Provinces, which are Prohibition Territories where whisky is forbidden, I went into the next car to ours for a drink of water. There was a little boy, about ten years old, there with his father and mother, and it is evident he had heard them speaking about it being forbidden to introduce spirits into Assinaboia and Alberta. So after he had taken a furtive and somewhat awe-stricken look at my hat, which, I am bound to say, was of extremely formidable brim, with the leather gear on it so much affected by Southern cow-boys, he turned to his father, saying, 'Pa, if the police knew a *cow-boy* had whisky, do you think they would search *him*?' Of course the little fellow thought the hat a sure sign of a desperate character, whose belt was certainly full of six-shooters and bowie-knives, and whose mind ran on murder and scalping.

At Moose Jaw, where we remained for some few minutes, there were a number of Cree Indians, bucks and squaws, some of whom came begging to us. These were the reddest, most bronzy Indians I ever saw. They used, I believe, to be constantly at war with the Blackfeet, who live nearer the Rockies.

I paid but very little attention to the scenery as we passed through the North-West Provinces, though it is not so wearisome as the Manitoban dead levels, on account of the prairie being somewhat rolling, with numerous lakes upon it, the haunt of flocks of wild fowl. But the country is uninhabited. It seems to me that we passed over nearly 600 miles of plain without seeing a town or any habitation save a few small houses of the section gangs. Of the millions of buffaloes that used to be on these prairies there are no signs save bones to be seen. In the United States they have about 300 head in the Yellowstone Park, and it is said there are a few on the Llano Estacado, or Staked Plain, in Texas and New Mexico. Some exist, too, in Northern Montana and Southern British Columbia, in the most inaccessible ranges, for the process of hunting selection has destroyed all on the prairie and given rise to a mountain variety. I confess, for my own part, that I have never seen one wild in all my wanderings.

At Gleichen we were told we could see the Rockies,

and I was so eager to get beyond the vile monotony of the prairie that I had my head out of the window all the while for hours before we got there. And I and Mac were now rather in straits. Our food supply gave out after two days, and this was the middle of the third. I had foolishly given a meal to a man who had nothing with him at all, and we were now suffering ourselves, staying our increasing appetites with tobacco. It does not, I imagine, predispose one to revel in heroic scenery for one's baser mechanism to go in pain and hollowness; but perhaps I had arrived at a stage of ascetic ecstasy, for I hardly thought of such needs the whole of that day, and was content in hunger until night blinded my vision and brought my soaring spirit back to its more material casing.

At Gleichen I could just discern the first faint line of the far Rocky Mountains, hung like a bodiless cloud in the air over the level plain. As we ran farther west it grew by slow gradations more and more distinct, until at last the sharp, fine, jagged outline stood out clear against the blue. Yet underneath that line was nothing, not even the ghost of the huge solidity of mountain walls. It was still thin, impalpable as faint motionless smoke, yet by the steadfastness of peak and pinnacle a recognised awful and threatening barrier.

We came to Calgary, a flourishing and well-known town. Here numerous Blackfeet had their teepees, or wigwams. I shook hands with two of this tribe, the most noble of the Indians. Two tall old men they were, one with smooth, tight skin and glittering eyes, calm, steadfast, and majestic; the other cut and carved by a million wrinkles, but strong and upright, with a kindly smile. Ye two of the Indians who pass away, I salute you! *Vos morituros saluto!*

Before Calgary we had crossed the Bow River, swift and blue, and heavenly and crystal, born of the mountains and fresh from snowfield and glacier. As we left the town we ran on the right bank, and being now among the first of the lower hills which buttress up the mountains from the plain, we went more slowly up grade, looking down into the stream far below. The sun was shining, the air clear and warm, the flowers blooming on every earthy spot, and the grass yet green.

In a few hours we ran up to the real entrance of the Bow Pass. Tired of straining my neck out of window, I left the passenger-car and climbed on to one of the freight-cars in front, and, spite of choking smoke, cinder and ash, I kept my place till we ran into the heart of the mountains and night as well, for I wished to be alone with the hills.

It was the first time in my life that I had seen mountains. I had been in Cumberland, it is true, and seen Skiddaw; I had climbed Cader Idris, and had lain there for hours, watching the vast stretch of sea and river and mountain; I had been on the Devon hills and on Derbyshire's peak. But these are not mountains of snow and fire perpetual. They are, it may be, haunted with ancient legend, but their newer garments of story and fable have clothed their primæval nakedness. We love them, but have no awe of them. They are not sacred. But the untouched virgin peaks of snow, the rocky pinnacles where eagles sun themselves in swift and icy air, the dim and scented pine-woods, the haunt of bears, the gorges of glaciers, and the birthplace of rivers, these are sacred. If I come to a solitude and say, 'Here man has not been,' if I can say, 'That rosy peak no eye has ever viewed but mine, who can reverence its glory,' then that place is indeed sacred, though an awe may be on me that at first precludes passionate love, permitting only adoration.

We are thousands of feet above the plain. Look back, and look your last on the vast and hazy prairie beneath you! In a moment you shall have passed the barrier and be among the hills, you shall be within the labyrinth and maze. Here is a vast gorge, now broad with sloping bastions of opposing fortresses on either hand, now narrow with steepest walls and impending rocks threatening the calm lakes that catch their shadows and receive their reflections. Even as you look do they not nod with possible thunderous avalanche, or is it the play only of shadow from opposite peak and pinnacle? How these are cut and scarped to all conceivable fantasy of art and inconceivable majesty of nature, how they are castled and upheld with arch and bridge and flying buttress! This is the aisle of the Great Cathedral of the Gods; this is the cave of Æolus, the home of the hurricane; this is the lofty spot most beloved by the sunlight, for here come the first of the day beams, and here they linger last on rosy snow covering the rock whose massy base lies in the under shadow.

I was in a land of phantasm, and the memory remains with me as a broken dream of wonder. As I write I catch from that past day shifting pictures, and, half seen, one dissolves into the next to give way in turn in the kaleidoscope to some other symbol of the seen. For memories of such a pageant as a man sees only once in a lifetime are but as conventional signs and symbols for the painting of the unpaintable, of the foam and thunder of the stormy seas, of the golden sunset, of the fleece of floating cloud. So we ran on into the night, and I slept with eyes and imagination jaded, at the end of our journey on the western slope of the Great Divide of the Continent, where the waters ran towards the set of sun.

It is almost as painful to me as I write to come back again to the more sordid facts of my journey as it was to be hungry. The troubles we pass through vanish from our memories and the pleasures remain, as the gold is caught in the sluice box while the earth and mud run out in turbid rush of water. Now I love to think only of the beauty I saw, and the pain drops away from me as I dream my toils over again. But the pain was real then.

On the morning when we woke in the Rockies we found ourselves at the end of the track. We had come nearly as far as the rails were laid, and quite as far as the passenger-cars were allowed to run. Round me I saw the primæval forest torn down, cut and hewed and hacked, pine and cedar and hemlock. Here and there lay piles of ties, and near them, closely stacked, thousands of rails. The brute power of man's organised civilisation had fought with Nature and had for the time vanquished her. Here lay the trophies of the battle.

The morning was clear and glorious, the air chill and keen, and through it one could see with marvellous distinctness the farthest peaks and the slender pines cresting the shoulders of the hills 3,000 feet above us. Before us stood the visible iron symbol of Power Triumphant—the American locomotive. She was ready to run a train of cars with stores of all kinds ten miles farther on, and now her whistle screamed. Echo after echo rang from the hills as the sound was thrown from one to the other, from side to side in the close valley, until it died like the horns of Elfland. We were to go with her, and all clambered in. Some sat on the top, some got in empty cars, with the side doors open. I was in one with about twenty others. I sat down by the door, opened my blankets and put them round me, for the cold grew more intense as we moved through the air and watched the panorama.

By this time I was absolutely starving, as it was now the third day since I had had a really satisfactory meal, and from Calgary to the Summit I and Mac had eaten nothing. So we were glad when our train stopped and let us alight. We were received by a man who acted as a sort of agent for the company. He got us in group and read over the list of names furnished him by the conductor of the train, to which about a hundred answered. He then told us we were to go much farther down the pass, and that we should have to walk about forty miles, and that we could get breakfast where we then were for twenty-five cents. It was about time to speak, and, as nobody else did, although I well knew there were dozens with no money in the crowd, I stepped up and wanted to know what those were to do who had no money, adding that I and my partner were 'dead broke.' And after this open confession of mine the rest opened their mouths too, until at last it appeared the moneyed members of the gang were in a very small minority. Our friend agreed that we couldn't be expected to go without food, and we had our meals on the understanding that the cost was to be deducted from our first pay. We had breakfast and set out on our forty miles tramp down the Kicking Horse Pass.

CHAPTER VI.

THE KICKING HORSE PASS.

I HAVE said there were about a hundred of us, and soon we were all strung out in a long line, each man carrying blankets and a valise, and some of us both. I had had in earlier days some experience in travelling, and took care not to overburden myself, as so many of the others did, who were on their first tramp; for the ease with which it was made possible to leave the crowded cities of the East, combined with the hard times, had brought a miscellaneous throng of men to British Columbia, many of whom had never worked in the open air, but only in stores and shops, whilst there were many who had never worked at all. It was quite pitiful to see some little fellow, hardly more than a boy, who had hitherto had his lines cast in pleasant places, bearing the burden of two valises or portmanteaus, doubtless filled with good store of clothes made by his mother and sisters, while the sweat rolled off him as he tramped along nearly bent double. Perhaps next to him there would be some huge, raw-boned labourer whose belongings were tied up in a red handkerchief and suspended to a stick. I had a light pair of blankets and a small valise, which Mac carried for me, as he had nothing of his own. My blankets I made up into a loop through which I put my head, letting the upper part rest on my left shoulder, the lower part fitting just above my hips on the right side. This is by far the most comfortable and easy way of carrying them, save in very hot weather.

We tramped along, Mac and I, cheerfully enough, very nearly at the tail of the whole gang, as we were in no hurry, and were yet somewhat weak. Presently Mac picked up with another companion, leaving me free to look about me without answering his irresponsible chatter or applauding his adventures in Wisconsin, where it appears he had very nearly killed some one for nothing at all, while he was drunk, as usual when not working.

I am fain to confess that my memories of the next two days are so confused that, whether Tunnel Mountains came before the Kicking Horse Lake or whether it didn't, whether we crossed one, two, or three rivers before we got to Porcupine Creek, whether it was one mountain fire we saw or two or more, I can hardly say with any certainty. All was so new and wonderful to me that one thing drove the other out of my head, and when I think it was so while I was walking slowly, I am lost in astonishment to see so many fluently describe mountain passes they have traversed in the train. I am afraid the guide-books must be a great aid to them.

Tunnel Mountain was more like a gigantic cliff than a mountain. One could see the vast rock run up perpendicularly till it passed above the lower clouds. High from where I stood, perhaps 3,000 feet above me, was a thin white line, which I was told was a glacier 300 feet thick. A thousand feet above us, small and hard to be distinguished against the grey-brown rock, were men working with ropes round them at a vein of silver ore. How they had gained such a position I cannot think, and how they maintained it, working with chisel and mallet in the keen air and frost of that elevation, is a greater puzzle. They must have looked down and seen us crawling on the ground like ants. The roar of the river, though at places it almost deafened us, must have been like a bee's murmur to them, and when the crash of a large blast hurled the rocks into the stream the report would come as a distant smothered roar.

The short tunnel ran through the outside of this cliff, and, just beyond, a roaring tributary of the Kicking Horse River made a bridge necessary. This was not finished then, but it had to be crossed, for there was no other way. It was sufficiently perilous. Along the cross-pieces of the bridge lay the stringers, pieces of timber 8 inches by 12 inches by 16 feet; these were set on their 8-inch side, two together on each side of the bridge, each couple at varying distances, sometimes close together and sometimes running so far apart one could scarcely straddle them. And these were not bolted down, but were loose and trembling. This was the path across! Had one fallen nothing could save him, especially if heavily burdened, for there were but the large lower timbers to catch hold of, and underneath, fifty feet below, sharp rocks and a roaring stream of water.

At one place we came to a river or large creek running over a flat with a very swift current, but still not boisterously or with any huge rocks in it. As the road ran into it on one side and emerged on the other, we could see it was fordable. But still no one seemed to like the prospect of wading through a stream whose current might be strong enough to carry a man off his legs and the water of which was icy cold. One by one the stragglers came up, until nearly our full band was congregated on the river banks. We looked for some wagons to come by, but could see none. At last, after trying in vain to persuade some of the others to venture in, I took off my trousers, boots, and socks, and with these hung round my neck I waded into the water. It was bitterly cold, especially as it was now a warm day with pleasant air and sun, and the stream washed against me so that I had to lean up against the current. The others stood watching me, giving me an occasional word of encouragement or a yell of delight at my strange appearance. After a considerable struggle I emerged on the farther bank in a red glow. But my luck in another way was bad. Just as I got out a wagon came round the corner to meet me, and in it was a woman—about the only one we had seen since we had left the summit or the end of the track. She burst into laughter at the ridiculous cranelike figure I cut, standing with my garments and long boots hung about me. I turned and sat down in the grass and made myself decent as soon as possible. In the meantime, much to my disgust, some wagons came up and carried the other men across. I had all my trouble for nothing, and my glorious example was lost on the crowd. After going another couple of hundred yards we came again to a wide stream, and this time I was myself carried over. And then we had a long tramp along the verge of a big mountain fire, which was crackling and smouldering from the banks of the river to the mountain tops.

At nightfall, or rather just before it, we came to the Porcupine Creek, another furious tributary of the main river, and here we had supper at one of the railroad camps. Afterwards we set about lighting fires for our camping-ground, for we had but the shelter of the pines that night. We dragged brush and sticks together, and borrowing some axes from the camp we cut up some of the trees that had been thrown down by the wind in the winter or been felled by the men who made ties. Four fires soon lighted up our forest, and blue and purple flames shot up, singeing the pines and sending up sparks into the blackness overhead, where their branches touched each other a hundred feet above. I think those fires of mountain wood upon the mountain always burn with far more beautiful colours than those on plains and lowlands, for here only, in the heart of the fire, can one see the fiery red, and over are blue and purple interlacings and shootings of purest colour standing out against the dark background of balsam and hemlock, while the curling smoke runs from violet to grey and shadow.

For an hour some of us flitted about in the darkness gathering in the firewood, and the rest lay down and smoked, or propped themselves quietly against the tree trunks, dreaming over the fire. It promised to be a chilly night. The crescent moon hung over a peak of snow, faint and new; but the stars were jubilant and strong, like glittering sword points in the deep transparent sky. Already behind the trees, where the shadows from the fires threw umbra and penumbra on the grass, were varying degrees of silvery frost, glittering brightly on the darkest umbral cone in the moonglow, and in the lighter shadow only chilling and stiffening the slender, infrequent grasses and the matted bundles of sharp pine needles. Close at hand, on the border of the pines, the creek ran over a bed of rounded boulders, here and there broken by a higher rock that threw a jet of foam in air. It ran rapidly and hurriedly by, with its shriller song all but overpowered in the deep strong bass of the distant river of roaring cataract. Beyond the creek, in its own shadow, for the moon's peak of silver snow showed above the barrier, was the sombre forest, at first a wall of solid blackness, breaking gradually with prolonged sight into lighter brush and black trunk below, with grey shadows and hollows over these, and above again lighter and lighter shades then ran to slender tracery against the blue, with here and there one star glittering through the branchy oriel windows to the sky.

I woke at midnight and found it sharp frost. The fires had burnt to embers. Round about me in every direction lay my companions sleeping, save one or two unfortunates without blankets, who kept their backs against the trunks of the pines and their heads and arms upon their knees, crouching in a heap to keep what heat they could in them, as they looked into the fires and wished for day. I walked out of the shadows of the forest to the banks of the creek. The moon was sunk deep below the sloping shoulders of her peak, and her pale fires had died from the snow and ice. The stars glittered more radiantly in a darker blue, and pine-wood and mountain shadow melted into one upon the distant slopes. Looking down the valley was vague darkness, and when I walked a few yards from the rushing creek I could hear plainly the wavering roar of the river palpitating musically through the calm cold air. Save that, there was no sound; everything was sleeping; and when I turned away from the look of the red eyes of fire that gleamed through the brush from our camping-ground, I might fancy myself alone, with the voiceless spirit of the mountains brooding over me, one with the night.

But the romance of the time fell from me as I felt the air more and more chilly, and I went to sleep again with my commonplace partner Mac, whose ideal was, I doubt not, a whisky bottle and nothing to do.

Next day another twenty miles through the great gap torn in the forests for the right of way of the railroad. The trees were hewed down, sawed and hacked in pieces, and piled on either side, dragged by horses or cattle. Cedar, white and red, fragrant balsam, dark hemlock, the sheltering spruce—all the pride of the forest went down before axe and saw for man's triumph. Grey and red squirrels came peeping to see what was being done in their troubled homes, and the striped chipmunks ran and darted here and there quicker than birds. We left the broad track and took the road, narrow and dark. Here one wagon could travel, but another could not pass it. It was a way hewn out of the primæval forest; it was full of stumps and holes, with pools of water here and there, and sloughs of mud enough to engulf a horse. Ruts were a foot or two deep. When a wagon met me I would climb on a log or squeeze into the brush while it went plunging by, threatening to drop to pieces with every shock, creaking and complaining as for want of oil. Yet the loads were not heavy, and the horses, for the most part, good and well cared for. On this 'toat' or freight-road the wagons went east during one part of the day and west during the other.

At noon on this second day we came to the 'Island,' a kind of flat just above the river, and far below where the track ran. The work here was of a severe character, as they made a 'fill' or embankment eighty feet high, I should think, or possibly much more. We scrambled down the end of this and went to get dinner at the camp on the Island. Up to this time they had always given us our meals in the tents with knives and forks and plates, but here the cooks brought out a huge can of soup, some potatoes, great lumps of boiled beef, and a pile of plates and a bucket of knives and forks. A chorus of growls rose up from us on all sides. A cry was raised for our friend the agent, who came out to view the scene. Some of us pointed out that, if we were to pay for our meals, we expected to be treated in a reasonable manner, and not like hogs. Some of the 'boys' said it was a regular 'hand out,' and that we looked like a crowd of old 'bummers.'

'Bummers' is American for beggars, and a 'hand out' is a portion of food handed out to a bummer or a tramp at the door when he is not asked inside. The agent looked as if he would like to say it was good enough for us, but the crowd was too big, and too ugly in temper, to play tricks with, and he temporised, calming us down; and finally, finding that we were not to be appeased, said we need not pay for it, if we ate it or not. We were hungry, however, and, finding it impossible to get a spread, we had to make the best of it; and soon all of us were fighting for knives and plates and spoons and soup. We sat round in groups, growling and eating like a lot of bears.

After dinner we started out again, passing every half-mile or so a railroad camp; and now we began to leave at each place some of our number, whenever any of the contractors were in need of more men. Mac and I were told with some others to stay at Ross and M'Dermott's camps; but when we got there, for some reason or another we did not like the look of the place, and concluded that we would take things into our own hands and go farther on. After leaving this camp we came to Robinson and Early's, and next to the large camp at Corey's, where they were making a tunnel through blue clay. This was called the Mud Tunnel. We passed on a little farther, and came to a sub-contractor's. At this point we met the agent, who had gone ahead of us on horseback. He reined up and said:

'Didn't I tell you fellows to stay at Ross and M'Dermott's?'

'Yes,' answered Mac.

'Well, why didn't you?'

'Oh, we didn't care about that place.'

'What do you want then? If you go on any farther I can't give you any more meals.'

I myself did not care about going any farther, and said so.

'Then you can work at Corey's if you like.'

I turned to Mac and said, 'Come, Mac, what's the good of fooling; come with me.'

'No back tracks, Texas. I'll stay here.'

It was settled finally that these should stay and work with the sub-contractor, and I went back to Corey's with the agent. When I got there it was dark and supper was over. I had a little to eat, and slept that night in one of the dining-tents, under the table, while above slept a New Brunswicker named Scott, who was to be my greatest friend hereafter both in British Columbia and California. He has often told me since that my last words that night were: 'I go to sleep to-night, lulled to slumber by the music of the Kicking Horse.'

CHAPTER VII.

THE RAILROAD CAMPS.

OUR camp was right on the banks of the river, which ran in a sharp curve round the base of the hill through which the tunnel was being cut. The Kicking Horse was furious as usual there, rushing at the rocks which impeded its course and breaking about them in foam, or leaping with a swing and a dive over the lower and more rounded boulders. Beyond it, on the other bank, was a thick wall of pine and fir, and overhead the vast slope of mountain. Our side was decorated with a medley of various-shaped tents, round and square and oblong, so that it was difficult at night for a stranger to avoid tripping himself up with the pegs and ropes, or half strangling himself with the stays carried from the ridge-poles to the trees growing about all the encampment. Besides the tents there were two large log-huts or shanties, built out of half-squared timbers with the bark only partly removed, and up a little slope, on the other side of the road which ran through the camp, stood a little log-house and kitchen for the accommodation of some of the 'bosses' and the head contractors. Beyond this the hill ran up gradually into a maze of fallen timber, with one little melancholy cleared space, where a simple and rude grave held the body of an unknown and friendless man who had been killed some little time before I came. And still farther on was the summit of the low hill under which the tunnel was to be, and above again mountain piled on mountain.

There must have been a hundred or more men employed at this work, which was of a hazardous and dangerous character. The hill was being attacked on both sides at once, and at the west end down stream the tunnel was advanced to some distance, but at the east end, though there, too, the hole had been run into the hill, the work was to do over again, owing to the tunnel having 'caved' in, in spite of the huge timbers. The hill was composed of gravel on the top, then a thick stratum of extremely tenacious blue clay, and beneath that lay a bed of solid concrete which required blasting. I and my new friend Scott went to work at the east end with a large number of others. We had to remove the immense mass of clay and gravel which had come down when the 'cave' had occurred, and to cut back into the hill some distance until it appeared solid enough for the new tunnel to be commenced. As the cut into the hill was now very deep, we worked on three 'benches.' The lowest and farthest out from the crest of the hill attacked the clay at the bottom; the next, twenty or thirty feet above us, cut into the loose gravel, taking it in barrows to each side; and the highest gang above that again wheeled away the sand at the top and cleared out the stumps as they came to them. The highest gang worked in comparative safety; the next in some peril, as they had to look out for the rocks that might fall in their own bench and for those from the upper bench as well; but the lowest gang were in danger of their lives all the time, as from both benches above them came continually what rocks escaped the vigilance of those working over their heads. I worked here myself, and without any exaggeration I can say I never felt safe, for every minute or so would come the cry, 'Look out below!' or 'Stand from under!' and a heavy stone or rock would come thundering down the slope right among us. I had been working three days, and on the third day a rock about a foot through, weighing perhaps 80 lb., came over without anyone crying out till very late. It came down and seemed to be about to drop right where I stood, so I made a prodigious jump on the instant, without having time to see where I was going, and struck my right knee under the cap on the end of a wheelbarrow handle just as the stone buried itself in the ground where I had been standing. The pain was so great that I had to sit down for ten minutes or more, and when I got up I found I could scarcely walk, as the swelling was so great. It was with difficulty I got to the camp, and for five days I was unable to work. There was a doctor, paid I suppose by the company, who came along on horseback at intervals, and he gave me some liniment and told me to rest. During these days I used to eat and sleep and read what I could get, which was very little, so I was thrown back on my old friend 'Sartor Resartus.' Sometimes another man who was too ill to work would come and talk with me, and at times I would go to the banks of the river and watch the stream as it ran past in such a fury and haste to get to the Columbia. I was not now lodged in the tent, but in a curious kind of gipsy arrangement which had been built by another man before I came. It was made of hooped sticks set in the ground, and over these were spread pieces of old canvas and a big uncured bullock hide, which indeed served admirably to keep out the rain, but stank most abominably when it was hot. Here I used to lie, as it did not permit one to stand or indeed to do much more than crawl into it, and look out, having good vantage-ground to view both the river and the road. At night I would make a fire, and six or a dozen men would come round and spin yarns, dry their clothes, and rake out embers for their pipes. After a few days I felt well enough to make an attempt at work, but was really unfit for it, and so worked but a part of a day at a time till I felt all right. We were paid two dollars and a quarter for ten hours, and had to pay five dollars a week for board. They did not make us pay for the lodging, as may be imagined.

On the Sunday after I felt quite well, I and a young Englishman, Tom, who shared my hide-tent, went for a climb. We walked a mile up the river, and turned off the road up a creek which ran directly from between two lofty peaks, both of which were above the line of perpetual snow. We walked for a while on the side of the creek, stumbling among fallen timber and brush, until at last it was such a thicket on both sides that it became impossible to advance a step, and we took to the water, stumbling on the slippery stones, sometimes getting into holes up to our knees. It was a steep climb. After making our way up about a thousand feet we came to an impossible-looking place. The creek had cut deeply into a slatey bed, and the sides were so steep and slippery that our first attempts were unsuccessful. We tried to go round, but the tangle of brush was so dense that it would have taken us an hour's work with the axe. Back we went to the foot of the little fall, and by scrambling like cats we got up, wondering how we were ever to get down. We still went on, finding it grow steeper and steeper, until at last it was almost like climbing up a cascade. I was in a profuse perspiration, and was kept damp by the spray. At last we came near to the top of the timber-line, where the creek branched into three. On our left hand, through the few trees, rose the loftiest peak, cut into pinnacles and deep gorges, and in these lay the glaciers, and on the rocky slopes was a thin covering of new snow that had been rain in the valley beneath us. Right from the highest peak to our feet ran a tremendous slope of crumbling fragments of the mountain, a 'rock slide' 2,000 feet high, while on each side was a fringe of lessening pines and scrub that failed at last from the bare rock, which left no foothold. In front was another peak, and on the left another, both bare save for glaciers, and glittering in the sun.

We turned and went back. My companion ran much faster than I, for I was afraid of hurting my knee, as I found it more tender descending than ascending. So in a few moments I was left alone, as he would not wait. When I got to where the difficult place was I was puzzled. Had I been quite well I could have managed it, but to make anything of a jump was impossible, and I could not get down without jumping. I should have been in a nice position if I had sprained my knee. I might have been eaten by bears before Tom would have thought of getting anyone to look for me. So I sat down and considered. There was lying in the middle of the verge of the fall a pine, from which branch and bark had long been stripped. Its lower extremity was about sixty feet away beyond the rocky pool where the water fell. The whole trunk was slimy and slippery with green water moss, as the spray kept it always wet. At first I did not think it possible to go down it, but the more

I looked at the way I had come up the more feasible the tree looked, until at last I concluded I must try it, hit or miss. I waded into the water, straddled my tree, and backed over the edge of the fall. The spray flew up and nearly blinded me, and my slide was such a slippery one that it took all the grip in my legs to keep me from going down at breakneck speed. I put the brakes on with my hands too, and gradually crossed the boiling pool, until at last the trunk got too big for me to hold on to, and I slid the last ten or twenty feet with a rush that landed me on my back in the shallow water. I had cleaned off the weed on the tree, but I had to get a stick to scrape myself down with. The rest of the walk home was easy after that.

Scott, whom I mentioned at the end of the last chapter, had meantime been discharged by one of the foremen, who considered he did not do enough work. He went to work for Robinson and Early, who were near at hand. It was now nearly time for me to go. On this my last day at Corey's I was working on the top bench with five or six others, who were some of the laziest men I ever saw. The foreman was not with us all the time, having to look after the men below, and when he turned his back, down would go a wheelbarrow and one would sit on it, while another would lie in the gravel. So, perhaps, only two or three would be doing anything. This day, however, as we were working right at the top of the slope, grubbing out stumps, it was impossible for all of them to hide at once. So they made up for this by doing as little as they could while pretending to do a great deal. I am not praising myself when I assert that I was really doing more work at that time than any one of the others, yet I was the one picked out for censure by the same foreman who discharged Scott. I was angry at this of course, and left work at 9.30, having worked a quarter of the day.

This camp was not a very nice one to work at. For one thing there were too many men, and it was so broken up with day and night shifts that one never knew where anyone else was working, and scarcely where he himself would work next day. Then the accommodation was so bad, and the cooks so pressed that they found it impossible to give the men their 'pie.' This piece of daily pastry is a source of wonderful content to many working men. Without it, let the other food be ever so good, he feels he is being defrauded, and with it, though it be only of dried apple and sodden paste, he will put up with no potatoes and bad beef, or even none at times. However, just before I left, the camp was split in two and two sets of cooks appointed, with the result that ours fairly gorged his men with pie. Instead of the usual solitary quarter, which one had to eye jealously or transfer at once to his own custody from the rusty tin plate, to keep some greedy man from getting two shares, whole pies were at the disposal of

G

every one, and there was great gorging and contentment.

On the whole, I was not sorry to leave; and that afternoon I walked up to Robinson and Early's, where Scott was, and was told by Early I could come up at once and go to work in the morning. So I packed up my blankets and walked up that evening in the dark. This camp was divided into two parts by the 'grade' or embankment where the rails would be laid. On one side were the dinner and cook's tents, the store tent, where one could get clothes and tobacco, the bosses' tents, and a big composite log and canvas building with bunks in it. On the other side were four neat little log-huts. I walked along the 'dump' or grade till I came to a fire where four or five men were sitting, and went down and joined them. Scott was not there. I did not know any of these men, but, of course, in a country such as this was, that would be no obstacle to my joining in the conversation. I soon found out that I should have to sleep in the big tent with a crowd of Finns and Italians. They told me that the 'grub' was good, that the bosses were not bad, though they made their men work hard. The wages were the same as I had been getting at Corey's.

I took my blankets and camped on a pile of balsam boughs in the lower bunks of the big tent. 'Bunk' is here but a euphemism for the ground, as bunk was divided from bunk by a six-inch log, with the bark and some of the smaller branches on, being nailed or tied against the uprights which supported the top tier. I made my bed in the dark and slept, covering my face over to keep the dust and dirt off that dropped through from the top bunk when the men in it gave a roll in their sleep.

Next morning I went to work 'picking on a slope,' that is, smoothing off the sides of the hill above the grade, as one sees it done in England when going through a railroad cutting. Scott was working near the camp among the rocks, where blasting was going on.

Surely the life I led for the next month was a strange one. I was working in the same glorious mountain scenery that had roused in me a fervour of artistic appreciation that had resulted in a curious state of forgetful ecstasy, blind and deaf to the actual around me. But now, while working, I became mechanical and base, the mountain opposite was painful, and I longed for a change of scene, an hour with the plain and prairie. Partly, no doubt, this change resulted from the strain put upon my imagination by the perpetual contemplation of the most magnificent scenery—a state of mind of which Ruskin speaks in the 'Modern Painters' when writing of the psychological effects of the various aspects of Nature— and partly from the manual labour, in its physiological effect of robbing the brain of the blood that ran to the active and strained muscles of perpetual effort. Perhaps it was also partly owing to the mental analysis and introspection which irksome toil forced me to, when I chanced to work alone or in circumstances which compelled my companions to silence. Long suffering from bodily ailments in London had induced, as it were, a morbid melancholy of mind, which remained even when the troubles of indigestion and bile were partially removed by the keen mountain air, and the sense of unfitness for my surroundings threw me back, when alone, into the morbid introspective lines of thought that had been my pain and solace in the solitary times of indifferent companionship at home. I would repeat to myself as I worked snatches of our melancholy modern poetry that I knew so well. The indictment of life in the 'Lotus Eaters' came before the Grand Jury of my passions and desires, and I found it a true bill. I smiled bitterly to myself to think of the gods, 'where they smile in secret,' and as I laboured I sang softly :

> Hateful is the dark blue sky, Vaulted o'er the dark blue sea;
> Death is the end of life. Ah, why Should life all labour be?

Yet, with the strange contradictions of man's nature, when I was with the others I was the merriest of all. There were some six or seven of us, English or American, who came together in one of the little log-huts, and we sang our songs and chatted and joked round the pine-wood fire that roared up the rude chimney, as if labour were but a dream, or, if real, a delight. There was Scott, little, with keen grey eyes, a reddish beard and moustache, light brown hair over a broad forehead that betokened untrained intellect, and a mouth which showed much possibility of emotion. He was not, in the ordinary sense of the term, educated, and was indeed ignorant in many ways, but he had that desire for knowledge which in so many goes farther than compulsory culture towards the attainment of mental height. After him in my mind comes Davidson, a Canadian also, a bricklayer by trade, but by no means to be judged by the standard of an English artisan of that grade. He had read a great deal in a desultory way, and was a man of kindliness and keenness of thought, though without possibility of culture such as Scott possessed. Then comes Hank, a rude, rough block of a man, uneducated, powerful, with sensual lips and mouth and rough shock of hair. He played an execrable fiddle most execrably, but his love for it and tolerance and gentleness forced forgiveness from me, even when the tortured strings drove me outside.

Another of our evening company was a pleasant Canadian, who also played on the violin, not so badly as Hank. He was somewhat melancholy, and I thought at times that some woman was at the bottom of his troubles. His name has slipped my memory, but I think it was Mitchell. There was also a German, Fritz, whom I shall speak of in the next chapter, as he was my companion in the journey towards the coast.

We were a strange gathering at night-time, and not without elements of the picturesque, I fancy, in our strange interior of log-hut and confused forms on blocks of wood before the fire, burning brightly, and throwing a glare on the darkness through the entrance, which did not boast a door, but only a rude portière of sewed sacks. We sang at times strange melancholy unknown ditties of love in the forests, songs of Michigan or Wisconsin, redolent of pine odour and sassafras, or German Liede, for we were more cosmopolitan than a crowd of Englishmen would be at home, and did not insist only on what we could understand. I myself often sang to them both English and German and Italian songs, and it seems strange to me now to think that those forests heard from me the strains of Mozart's 'L'Addio,' sung doubtless out of time, as it was also out of place perhaps, and the vigorous tune of 'La donna è mobile.' But even songs like these were appreciated, and often called for, with 'Tom Bowling' or some other English sea-songs. Then we would tell each other stories or yarns, and I would repeat some of my travels in Australia for them, or explain how large London was, or tell those who had never seen the ocean stories of my own and my brother's voyages, or those of the great English sea-captains.

Such evenings came to be a recognised institution, and if I felt melancholy or savage one or another of these men would come to the little tent I now had all to myself, and say they wanted me to settle some point in dispute for them. For now, by virtue of my education, which was apparent to them, they made me 'arbiter elegantiarum,' umpire and referee as to pronunciation, and encyclopædia, so that I was often hard put to it by a dozen different questions, which only a visit to a library could settle. I wrote for them a song which was very much admired as the culmination of genius. It was a song of the C. P. R., or Canadian Pacific Railroad, and all I remember is the chorus, which was—

> For some of us are bums, for whom work has no charms,
> And some of us are farmers, a-working for our farms,
> But all are jolly fellows, who come from near and far,
> To work up in the Rockies on the C.P.R.

From which specimen the reader will not estimate my poetical powers so highly as the simple railroad men.

Perhaps the most surprising incident to me during the month I worked at this camp was the unlooked-for appreciation of some lines which few ordinary educated people at home really like, through lack of finer insight. It happened one Sunday afternoon that I, Scott, Davidson, Hank, and Mitchell were in one of the 'shacks,' or huts, and they were idly listening to me while I was inveighing against the injustice in life, its vanity and uselessness. Nobody but Scott was paying much attention, as I thought, and turning to him I repeated Rossetti's last sonnet in the 'House of Life,' the 'One Hope.' To my surprise Mitchell asked me to say it again, and then made me copy out the first quatrain:

> When vain desire at last and vain regret
> Go hand in hand to death, and all is vain,
> What shall assuage the unforgotten pain,
> And teach the unforgetful to forget?

Surely it was a strange enough thing for Rossetti to come to my memory in this beautiful desolation, but it was stranger still that his sorrow should find an echo in the heart of a poor labourer, to whom we so usually deny the power of real suffering, and the spirit of appreciation of subtle rhythms and obscurer imagery.

Often after that I spoke to this man, feeling that to him had been given great power of suffering, or he could never have understood. I believe that, if the poets learn in suffering what they teach in song, we also must suffer greatly before we can learn of them.

Meanwhile, in the daytime there was the usual labour, such as drilling holes in the rock to blast it with powder, whose explosion sometimes threw the heavy stones a hundred yards into the torrent of the foaming river. We would dodge behind trees and get into all sheltered places till the shot was fired, then come out again and take away the *débris*, hammering the larger blocks to pieces and shovelling up the smaller into the carts. Then there would be slopes to make smooth and round rocks and stones to be picked up from the borders of the Kicking Horse, to make a 'riprap' or stone wall at the bottom of the embankment, where the river would chafe it when swollen with melted snow. It was often laborious and wearisome, and I never looked at the scenery then, except, perhaps, when clouds gathered overhead, and rain mist crawled along the ramparts of the hills, filling the valley, until a shower would come upon us suddenly and as suddenly depart, when the mountain wind rolled up cloud and mist and the sun shone bright upon the hills above, dazzling with a sheet of new snow that had fallen on us below as rain. Or sometimes at evening, especially on Sunday, which in our camp was an idle day, I would walk up the grade to the turn of the river, and see, perhaps, the most exquisite picture that remains in my memory. At my feet ran the tumultuous current of the river, swinging quickly with a loud murmur to my left, covered with short crisp waves, with here and there a hurrying swirl and breaking foam that showed a hidden rock. It came towards me for three hundred yards, it may be, showing a swift declivity from the mass of argent foam as it turned the bend where stood a knoll of noble pines. Across the stream from where I sat were larch and pine on a spur shouldering rapidly from the river to the mass of the main mountain. Its side was cut away steeply by the wash of water, and showed bands of coloured clay, and here and there was a solitary tree marking its lofty line against the mass of the hill, emphasising by its sombre foliage the red and yellow ground against which it rose and from which it sprang. And in front was the mountain itself, rising from its shadowy base, where the thick forest of green marked its foot against the foam of the rapid, to loftier height on height, whence the trees showed less and less, until they were at last but a faint fringe and sparse adornment of the line sharp against the sky, and higher still a peak of solitary snow, rosy in the sunlight that had left me in shadow for an hour.

If I walked but half a mile up the road I came upon another beautiful sight, for there the valley pass was broader, and had a long, almost level space, beyond which was one of the queen peaks of the Rockies, whose presence dominated many miles of the valley.

It was after one of these evenings spent alone with the mountains that I had a long talk with my companions as to what they proposed to do. Some intended staying on the railroad work until it was finished, and some thought of leaving it soon, and making their way into lower British Columbia over the intervening ranges of mountains. This had been my intention since leaving Corey's. It was quite impossible for me to stay at such irksome labour much longer, and I had tried to obtain what information I could as to the route. This was very sparse. There were vague reports as to the immense difficulties and dangers awaiting anyone rash enough to attempt it, and had I been very timid I should have been scared into staying in the Rockies for the winter. This I hated to think of, as the snowfall would be tremendous and the cold very severe at that elevation and latitude. There were four possible ways out. One was to go back through the North-west Provinces and Manitoba. This could not be thought of. For one thing, I hate going back at any time, and in America 'forward' was always my motto. Another objection was that one would have in all probability to walk great part of a thousand miles to Winnipeg, as it was reported that the train men had very strict orders to let no one 'beat' his way on the trains, and of course I had insufficient money to pay my fare, even if I had desired to do it. There was another exit from the mountains which commended itself to my imagination if not to my prudence. That was to make a raft and go down the Columbia to Portland, Oregon, or rather to Kalama, W.T., first, and then up the Willammette to Portland. A German at Corey's had told me that this was feasible. He swore that the Columbia was 'smooth wie a looking-glass,' and that there was no danger at all. Others, however, told me of the great falls of the Columbia and the rapids, and asserted there were so many terrible gorges and cañons and whirlpools to be passed through that the river took a Dantean and Infernal colour in my mind. And, worst of all, it was utterly impossible to get a good map. So this was laid aside as impracticable. The next way was to go down to the Columbia and take the 'trail' to Sand Point, on the Northern Pacific Railroad in Montana, a journey of 300 miles, which would take from fifteen to twenty days and require one to pack a large quantity of food on his back to provide for all possible accidents and delays. The remaining route was to follow the railroad line. This would lead me to the Columbia, then over the Selkirk Range by Roger's Pass, and over the Columbia again. As far as I could gather we should then be in some kind of civilisation. But this, as will be seen, was far from the truth. The fact of the matter is that I could find no one who had been the journey, and the reports about it were so contradictory that in the Kicking Horse Pass it was impossible to find out how far it was across the Selkirk Range, whether it was 60 or 120 miles or even more. There was a halo of romance thrown over the whole place west of us, and when we passed in imagination the Columbia for the second time all beyond was as truly conjectural as El Dorado or Lyonesse. But this was the route I determined to take at the end of September, when I proposed leaving the camp. But my departure was hastened by the following circumstance. I and some Finns and another Englishman had been set to work in a very wet and nasty place, from which we had to run the dirt in wheelbarrows over planks, and as the nature of the place necessitated our getting wet none of us liked it. About ten in the morning

Robinson, one of the contractors, came down to take a look at us, and while standing on the bank spoke sharply to my English companion, who answered him back with no less sharpness. Next time he ran the barrow out it capsized. He laughed, which infuriated Robinson, who ordered him peremptorily to take his barrow out of the way. The young fellow said, 'I don't *have* to, Mr. Robinson.' This made Robinson worse. He jumped down, grabbed hold of him, and, being a very powerful man, shook him to and fro as a terrier shakes a rat, at the same time threatening to strike him. This, however, he refrained from doing, and finally he ordered him to go to the camp and get his money. Of course this was nothing to do with me, but still I did not care to work for a man who had as little control over himself as the contractor showed, fearing that I might myself have a disturbance with him, which would end either in him or me being disabled ; so when noon came I went and got my time made up, and sold the order, which would not be cashed for nearly a month, to Davidson, the bricklayer. I went then to Fritz, the German, and persuaded him to come with me. I should much have preferred Scott or any of the others, but none would leave the work for a while, though some of them had it in their minds to go farther west before the snow blockaded them in. So I rolled up my blankets and found a nice tin-pot with a handle, which we should call a 'billy' in Australia, and stole a cup and knife and fork. The cook made us up some food in a parcel, and with our blankets on our backs we set off down the road. As I passed the men sang out: 'Good-bye, Texas, take care of yourself.' I shook hands with my particular friends as I met them at intervals on the mile of work taken by Robinson and Early, and set off into the unknown country with 18 dols., or a little over 4*l*. I saw my friend Scott the last of all as we turned the corner. But we were to meet again.

CHAPTER VIII.

THE COLUMBIA CROSSING.

FRITZ and I passed through Corey's camp, as it lay in our westward journey, and I was greeted, of course, by some of my old companions, who asked me where I was bound for. When I told them we were going across the Selkirks, many of them really seemed to think I might as well jump into the Kicking Horse. One said, 'Well, old man, if you really mean going, you must have lots of grit, but I'll bet you a dollar you will soon turn back.' I assured him that I was not going to come back, and that I would die on the trail first. We shook hands and parted.

We had from Corey's tunnel about fourteen miles to traverse before coming to the Columbia Valley and Golden City, which was at the mouth of the Kicking Horse Pass. Our way lay along the main and only road, first on the left and then on the right side of the river going down. Beautiful as the upper part of the pass is, I think that this last fourteen miles is in some ways even more delightful. We went for some miles by the side of the river, which foamed and thundered over huge rocks, and rushed through narrow openings to broaden out into foaming rapids. Then we began to ascend, as it had been impossible to take the road on a level without encountering the engineering difficulties of tunnel and rock cut, which made the railroad in this lower pass so costly. We went up and up the side of the hills, until at last we were probably a thousand feet above the river and the railroad track. Below us the stream was at times calm and blue and then instantly torn and fretted into foam. The road we were walking on was sufficiently wide for one wagon, but there was scarcely at any one place more than a foot or two to spare, and sometimes there was so little room that I had to scramble up the hill out of the way, or stand on the lower slope of crumbling stone, while a vehicle passed. Sometimes I saw that a horseman had to turn back for a hundred yards or more before he could make his way beyond the wagon; and the declivities were of such a steep character that, had the brakes given way at many places, horses, driver and wagon would have rolled a thousand feet below!

At last we began to go down, and came finally in sight of the valley of the Columbia. We could see the Kicking Horse quietly making its way across the long flat to the main river, and some miles away, under the heights of the Selkirk Range, we could catch a glimpse of the blue broad waters into which it ran. We turned from the road, taking a footpath which led us steeply down to Golden City. It was now evening.

Golden City is a beautiful and alluring name, but I scarcely think that its most ardent supporter would allow that it really deserved such an adjective. It consisted, when I saw it, of a few log-huts and a few tents. There were two or three stores, where goods of all kinds were sold; there were also several places in which spirits could be obtained, I should imagine, if one could judge by the amount of noise issuing from some of the habitations. There was also a blacksmith's shop, and a blacksmith who was fairly busy. It was at this town we proposed to buy our provisions for the journey, and here we made more inquiries in order to find out how far it really was across the Selkirks. At the blacksmith's we found the very man to make them of, as he was in the habit of going across the range sometimes, and was now getting ready for another trip. He tried to scare us into going with him, offering to take us for 10 dols. apiece, but finding that we meant going by ourselves he gave us what advice he could, and told us that the journey from Columbia to Columbia across the Big Bend was not more than seventy-five miles, and that we had yet to go eighteen miles to the north of where we were then before we came to the first crossing of the Columbia.

We went into a store and bought our provisions. Here is the list :—

Flour	.	.	.	10 lb.	Boston biscuit	.	.	5 lb.
Bacon	.	.	.	6 ,,	Baking soda	.	.	2 oz.
Tea	.	.	.	1½ ,,	Prunes	.	.	2 lb.
Hard biscuit	.	.	10 ,,	Butter	.	.	1 ,,

Of course we paid extraordinary prices, but I have lost my note of them. I think the bacon was twenty pence a pound, and, in such a place, of course it was not of very fine quality. For reasonably good tea we paid 3s. 9d. a pound.

We walked three miles north, and camped a few yards from and above the road in a pine-wood. Fritz, who was the more active member of the two, did the cooking, though I made and attended to the fire. I have often noticed when travelling how one's companion alters one's self. In Iowa and Minnesota, when with Ray Kern, I did everything and was most active. Now, with Fritz, I was the lazy member of the firm. We, however, did not do much cooking that night, beyond making tea, for we had cooked provisions with us from the camp. After supper I lay back against a pine, smoking dreamily and looking out across the valley at the great barrier of the Selkirks, which rose like a wall beyond the river. In the advancing shadow of the evening the lower hills were dark, for the sun was setting behind them. In this darkness the black solidity seemed perpendicular, but above, the indentations of the valleys could be seen, and over these were the snow-capped summits piled one on another. As far as one could see on either hand this wall extended, and just half-way from sunwhite crest to shadowy base hung long white cloud wreaths, motionless and sullen, just catching on their upper sides a faint glow from the sunlight that yet remained on the peaks. And as I lay the light faded away, the hills took deep violet and purple hues, and they were deep and transparent as the darkest amethyst.

I think that hour I spent watching the changes of light and shadow on those unchanging hills was the most peaceful of all my life. There seemed then in life nothing more of sorrow than gentle melancholy, nothing more of passion than lives in kindliest memory, and no more pain at all. Then, if ever for one hour in my restless life, I was at rest.

I slept that night the sleep of the righteous, on a spot where the turf seemed soft and dry, from which I removed the little sticks and branches of decaying wood that dropped from the trees above me. The scent of the pine smoke of our dying fire mingled with the sweet native odours of the place, making a pleasant incense smell. In the morning I woke when the first grey dawn was on the opposite hills, and as I rolled over and put my head out of the blankets I saw a little red squirrel sitting with his brush over his head gnawing a crust of bread. It was, may be, his first taste of that civilisation whose last word to such is shooting and skinning or a cage, after blithe woodland freedom. Here and there a bird or two chattered overhead or in the lower brush, preparing for flight, and down the valley came sounds of other life awakening—the neigh of a pack-pony or the bray of a mule from the corrals of the Golden City. From the river light wreaths of mist arose and gathered with advancing day upon the hills, from whose crests the rapid sunbeams ran to their bases, discovering the huge gaps and gorges hidden from sight the evening before. For it was day now, and time for breakfast.

Our simple meal over, and the embers of our relighted fire extinguished or but smouldering, we made up our burdens. It was decided that I should carry both sets of blankets, which would weigh about 16 lb., and the 10 lb. of flour, and Fritz took the remaining provisions. We were then about equally burdened, each carrying about 26 lb., which was no small handicap, considering the country we had to travel over. We both had plenty of matches, and I, for additional precaution, took a small medicine-bottle with me filled with lucifers and tightly corked. I had experienced in Australia the misery of camping out without a fire, and I had no desire to make perhaps a week or ten days' journey on raw bacon and flour if an accidental swim in a river or a heavy fall of continuous rain should deprive us of the power of making a fire.

Our way now ran north, still following the line of railroad work, to where it was to cross the Columbia, eighteen miles from the Golden City. The grading was here of an easy character, as it was a low embankment that could be made of the recent sands and clays of the valley alluvium; consequently it was let out in great measure to small parties of working men, or 'station men' as they are called, who were paid by the piece and not by the day. The only difficulty here was the number of little bridges that would have to be built, owing to the swamps and back-washes from the Columbia, for this part of the valley was absolutely flat. For part of the time we walked along the road, and then along the grade if it seemed easier and more direct. About half-way to the Columbia, however, we found ourselves in rather an awkward place. The grade ceased abruptly on the edge of a deep sheet of water that had previously run alongside of it on our right hand between us and the road for a mile or more. It was necessary either to get across or go back. We searched for some time before we found a place that seemed fordable, and that was rather doubtful. However, anything seemed preferable to going back, and I stripped myself nearly to a state of nature and waded in, holding clothes and blankets and flour above my head. At the deepest it was only breast high, so I arrived without mishap at the other bank, and was presently joined by Fritz.

Early in the afternoon we came to the Columbia Crossing, where there was a rather lively canvas town, consisting of numerous stores and saloons and gambling-houses. We passed through it and went down to the river, which was here of no great breadth, though strong and deep. We were ferried over for twenty-five cents apiece, and in a few minutes stood on the rude road in the thick forest. We were at the foot of the Selkirks.

CHAPTER IX.

THE TRAIL ACROSS THE SELKIRKS.

WE were still on the wagon road, if road it can be called, which was all stumps and rocks and hollows, swampy and thick with mud. It ran steeply enough up the mountain, through pine, balsam, hemlock and birch, past a few railroad camps, for the first work on this side of the river had been commenced some time. As we walked we could hear below us the thunder of the blasting, and could catch now and then sight of a wreath of powder-smoke among the trees as it eddied upwards. We came out at last, after a hard climb, to where it was possible to get a view of the river and Death Rapids. We were almost above it, and as we looked down we could see the high walls of rock on either side and the dark blue water before it broke. This cañon has some dangerous whirlpools in it, and I was told of many accidents which occurred to men attempting to raft it. Two young fellows on a raft were drawn into a whirlpool, both were sucked under, one never to reappear, while the other was thrown up before he became insensible, and, grasping a floating pine trunk, he was saved. Once the railroad men were going to raft some dump cars down the rapids; the raft broke away from them and ran the gauntlet of the rocks, and was brought to shore eleven miles below.

It was now getting towards nightfall, and it behoved us to seek out a camping-ground. About three miles from the river we came to a sharp bend in the road and a little gorge or cañon, down which leapt a creek that ran across the road and plunged into the valley. We saw a little clear space of velvet lawn ten yards from the road, and, scrambling across a pool upon a fallen tree, we laid our packs down and built a fire. We were in absolute darkness in a few minutes, for lofty rocks were round us and thick growth of pine and brush above. The spray from the fall leapt almost to where we made our beds, and the damp air and seclusion gave good growth to the ferns about us. It was with some trouble that we made a fire, as we had no axe with us. We cooked some bacon, boiled some tea, and with biscuit made a comfortable meal. Fritz's last words to me that night were: 'If you wake early call me, for I must steal an axe in the morning, for this is our last chance of getting one, as far as I can see.'

I called him at early dawn: 'Fritz, how about that axe?' And I turned over and went to sleep again. When I woke once more Fritz was making tea. I asked if he had got the axe. He pointed to my side, where it lay in the grass. He said: 'I went down this creek till I came to the camp, but I couldn't see one, so I walked right through to where they were working and picked this one up. It is a good one, but wants grinding. Now we must look for a grindstone.'

Of course I know the morality of this axe business is very questionable, but I lay all the responsibility on Fritz. He suggested it, and he stole it. It is true I had the benefit of it, but I couldn't help that.

We rolled up the blankets and set off as soon as possible. This day we passed the last contractors and entered on the loneliest part of the road. At a surveyor's camp we ground the axe and made it a useful weapon—in fact, improved it so much that we considered now that we had at least a part title to it. This day was the last day of comfort for me. The inevitable hardships of the journey I thought little of; but, unfortunately, my boots began to chafe me, and gradually I wore a raw place on both heels, so that I walked more than 130 miles, every moment in positive pain and anguish. I have at times in England considered a blister a thing intolerable, but when the blister gives way for a raw bleeding place about the size of a florin I think there is not much doubt that the former is preferable. In the evening we came to the Beaver Creek and crossed it, and following the road about a mile, after having had a talk with a hunter who had his camp at the crossing, we made ours under a thick balsam tree, cutting down another small one to make our bed of the branches. We were in tolerable loneliness. While Fritz made the supper, I, still being lazy partner, went to the banks of the creek and bathed my sore and aching feet in the cool running water, watching the sun set on the peaks by which the Beaver ran. We had a fine supper that night. We had bought fifty cents' worth from the cook of the last surveyor's camp we had passed, and for our money we got biscuits, cakes, deermeat, bread, and some fruit pie. So we made merry, and smoked the pipe of peace and contentment ; while I put away from me the thoughts of the misery I should endure in the morning when I put my boots on again.

But the morning came, and the misery had to be endured, although I put it off as long as possible, walking round barefoot till we were nearly ready to start. This is a bad plan, however, and in future I washed my feet, dried them, warmed the boots at the fire, and put them on the first thing. In this way they get supple, and are not so harsh and hard when one has to make a move. We started again, and walked through the thick forest on a reasonably level road that did not entail much climbing, until we came at last to the road-makers' camp. Here we saw a party of hunters, with black and grizzly bears' skins hung up, and I began to think there were other dangers, perhaps, to be encountered than those we had reckoned on. Our chief fear had been lest we should run out of provisions, not lest we ourselves should make provisions for a hungry grizzly; and we were badly armed, having nothing but the axe and my bowie-knife. However, it could not be helped; it was to be done.

After walking a mile we came finally to the end of the road, such as it was, and entered on the trail.

There were now three of us, for on this day at noon we came upon a man camped in a little bark 'lean-to' all by himself. He was suffering from an access of bile and blues, brought on by drinking heavily in Columbia City, and had dragged himself so far. When we came by he had been there two days, and as it was time to make dinner we stayed with him and used his fire. We had a talk with him, and finding him to all appearance a good possible partner, we asked him to come with us. This he was glad enough to do, as it was not by any means a nice walk for a man by himself. His name was Bill.

The trail upon which we were now walking was a narrow foot or bridle path cut years before through the forest. It had received very little attention since it was first made, and was blocked every now and again by trees that had fallen either by natural decay or by force of wind. At times it was full of large stones, requiring some circumspection in walking to avoid spraining one's ankle, or a mass of mud in which one sank a foot deep. The brush, heavy with rain and dew, dropped its moisture on us as we passed, and the prickly devils' clubs made things unpleasant for us as well.

At noon, or a little later, we passed through some hundreds of yards of swamp, in which I had to walk quickly and carefully to avoid getting 'bogged down,' and, in spite of all my care, when half across it I fell on my face and hands in the sticky mud, through my foot getting caught in a slender branch of willow trodden into it. I was a most melancholy-looking object, and Bill and Fritz exploded with laughter at my appearance, which was remarkable, no doubt, as on arriving on firm ground I had to scrape myself down with a knife and wash the mud out of my nose, ears, and eyes at the first creek.

Towards evening we were overtaken by a bright, smart-looking young fellow, who was well dressed, carrying an overcoat and no blankets. He was walking rapidly, and would have passed us had it not been near camping-time. After going a mile or two more we found a splendid place among a few trees in a fork of the creek, along the banks of which the trail ran, and right under a magnificent peak or crowd of peaks, which crowned an almost perpendicular wall of rock two or three thousand feet high. Under the trees we found a few sheets of bark leaning against a horizontal supported by two sticks, which would serve us as a shelter from any rain or dew. It was now getting a little dusk. Fritz set to work making a fire, Bill and our new friend sat talking, and I went down to the creek with the flour and baking powder to make some bread. It was necessary to get a mixing and kneading place. I suppose a civilised cook would find some trouble in bread-making under such circumstances, but I was equal to the emergency, and mixed my dough in the hollowed top of a rock, and kneaded it on another flat stone. By this time the fire was roaring, and I soon found enough ashes to bake it in. In Australia, under similar circumstances, we used to cut a square piece of bark out of a tree and mix the bread on that.

We cooked some bacon, making neat frying-pans of our tin plates, having cut sticks that were slightly bent at one end, which we split, to insert the edges of the plates; and we boiled the tea as usual. Fritz and I at Golden City had had an argument as to whether it was best to take tea or coffee. He wanted coffee and I tea. He had not travelled so much as I had, and I knew from my life in the Australian bush that tea was the best drink in the world when one is roughing it. It was not long before Fritz acknowledged I was right, and he was as eager as I to light the fire and 'boil the billy' whenever we stopped during the day.

That night was the last of pleasant times, and it was the best. On the morrow my sufferings were to commence in earnest. But here everything was delightful—the well-situated camp, the shelter, the trees, water brawling on either side; on the left the enormous wall of mountain with old glaciers here and there, and drifts of ancient snow, and snow bridges, under which ran the decreasing waters of approaching winter; on the right three sister peaks of lofty snow, and beneath them and all around the quiet yet murmuring forest. So we sat round the roaring camp fire, on which we piled all available logs, smoking and chatting and joking until the blaze shone its brightest in the full darkness of night and threw faint shadows and glows across the creeks into the forest on one side and the mountain on the other. Our new friend was a curious individual, who told us a number of stories calculated to make us respect his personal courage if they were true, and his powers of invention if they were false. For my part, I preserved my usual attitude in such cases—I believed as much as I could, rejecting the rest. In this way I obtain much more enjoyment from yarns than the cold, incredulous critic. My own opinion is that he was now in a hurry to get to a place where he was unknown. I fancied that the police on the railroad line might have a fancy to interview him. If I am wrong I beg his pardon, for he afforded me much entertainment by one story, the point of which consisted in his luck in stealing ten horses in succession, at each fresh capture leaving the horse he had wearied out as an exchange, without being captured until in the act of taking the tenth, when he was compelled to surrender to a loaded gun held by a man who turned out to be his brother-in-law! This story and another one about his throwing a British Columbia sheriff in the Fraser River, how he was captured, sentenced, imprisoned, and how he escaped, kept us well amused until it was time to turn in.

In the morning, after breakfast, he left us, as he could walk much faster than we, owing to his being unencumbered with blankets and much food. So we bade him farewell. This day we came across a splendid patch of huckleberries and blueberries, and putting our blankets down we all three ate solidly for about an hour. These huckleberries are to my taste the nicest wild fruit I have ever tasted, and bears are of the same opinion, being extremely fond of them.

My feet were now in a horrible condition, and the pain every step caused me was exquisite. I picked up a pair of boots that had been thrown away and tried to wear them, but found them even worse than my own. It was impossible to walk barefoot in such a country, or I would have tried it. It was simply a case for endurance, and I had to support myself with the knowledge that it could not last for ever. This day we passed the summit or highest point in the pass, which was a meadow of natural grass and rather swampy. Just after passing it, and coming to the streams that ran west, we found a poor pack-pony lying in a swamp unable to get up. He had been left behind as useless, I suppose; but it seemed a cruelty to let him die of starvation, so we pulled him out and put him on his feet, hoping he would manage to pick up a living. It was no infrequent thing now for us to find these ponies dead alongside the trail, and if what we heard was true one at least had been the means of saving the lives of some men who had attempted to cross the trail with insufficient provisions, for they had eaten part of it.

As I stumbled painfully along the trail, now the last of the three who was wont to be first, I overtook an old blear-eyed individual carrying an enormous pack nearly as big as himself. He was short and thick, with boots up to his hips and a cap down to his eyes. In his boot he carried a knife and in his belt an old muzzle-loading revolver. His weather-beaten and hairy countenance was devoid of joy or sorrow, and it seemed to me that his mind was a trifle weak. He camped with us that night.

It had been raining since the early morning, and we were sufficiently wet and miserable. If my feet had been sound such a trifle as rain would never have disturbed me, but when one is in positive anguish a little additional discomfort sometimes is the last straw. If it had been dry it would have been of no consequence where we camped, provided only that there was wood and water, and there are few places where there is not enough of one and too much of the other in this mountain range. But as it was raining it was positively necessary to find some shelter, and we walked for an hour after dark, stumbling and cursing, looking for a good tree. At last, just when we were about to give up and camp anywhere, rain or no rain, we came on a delightfully thick spruce fir close to the trail. This tree is the best shelter-tree in the world, I should think. In appearance it is something like a lofty pagoda, and the thick needles and downward slope of the branches throw off all rain, even if it be wet for weeks. We threw our blankets underneath, cut some of the lower branches of it off, and were in a dry circular tent, with a big pole in the middle to be sure, but a plentiful soft bed of generations of soft-shed needles. Outside we soon had a roaring fire, throwing a red light into the murky air and diffusing a pleasant warmth on all around, though the heavy rain quenched the outside embers and caught the floating sparks before they could rise a yard from the blaze.

I slept magnificently that night, 'forgetting my miseries, and remembering my sorrows no more.' But in the morning we had an unpleasant surprise. It seemed very bright when I opened my eyes, although I knew it must be still early by my sleepy sensations, and when I looked round I found it had been snowing heavily during the night, with the result that there were six inches of snow on the ground. The trail was covered by it, and it seemed as if we were in for a detention. However, it thawed rapidly, and most quickly on the bare trail, so that we were able to find our way with but little difficulty.

I

We were, as I have said, now well on the western slope, but instead of there being less climbing there was more. The path ran up one side of a mountain and plunged down again on the other, and this was the way with it all that day. The rain again commenced to fall, and the snow dropped from the trees on my head and down my neck, so that I was wet through in half an hour, and yet perspiring toiling up the steep slopes. And while going up my heels were torture to me, and when going down my boots, being now thoroughly wet, gave me blisters on the toes. The trail, too, was at times almost impassable for wind-fallen trees, as it is no light thing, when one is wet, weary, and heavily burdened, to climb over a dozen trees, three feet through, every hundred yards. And now, to add to our troubles, we came to a river which had to be crossed, the Illecilliwet. If we had come there a day or two before it might have been possible to wade it, but now, swollen with two days' rain and melted snow, on the side nearest to us it was five or six feet deep, and the current running eight or ten miles an hour made it impossible to attempt it. The only thing to be done was to fell a lofty tree and to trust to its lodging in the shallow water on the other bank, so that we could go over it as a bridge. We put our burdens down, and selecting a tree felled it in about three-quarters of an hour. It fell with a tremendous splash into the river, and we raised a shout of joy, seeing that it reached well across. But, alas, our joy was short-lived! Before we could get on to it the rapid current took hold of it, and slowly first, and then more quickly, it swung right down stream and lay along the bank on which we stood. There was nothing to do but to fell another. This time we selected a loftier red pine, and in another hour it crashed into the water, with its slender top lying on the dry stones of the farther side. I seized my blankets and the axe and ran out on the tree, and after me came Bill and Fritz. I scrambled through the branches half-way across, with them close behind me, and then slowly, but surely, the tree began to move and swing. I scrambled a yard or two more on the trunk, that was here in the water, and then made a jump into the stream on the upper side, the water coming over my long boots. It was icy cold, and it swept so strongly that it was impossible to go straight across, and so I was forced to go down stream, with difficulty preserving my balance on the boulders of the river bed. As I got ashore, with Bill and Fritz a moment later, the stream took possession of our bridge and swung it alongside the first tree. We had got over, and that was all.

We had left the old man behind, and I don't know how he got across, although I know he managed it, as I heard of him afterwards in Lower British Columbia. I met some time after this a man who, recognising him from my description, told me that he was known as 'the man-eater,' through his having eaten part of his companion, who, having been caught in the snow with him on the eastern slope of the Selkirks, had died from starvation and exposure.

We camped, soon after crossing this river, in a gloomy cedar forest. This is the worst shelter-tree in existence, I believe. Its scanty foliage and infrequent boughs make it little better than nothing at all, and indeed sometimes worse, as one may select unconsciously a spot to camp in where the branches deliver a concentrated stream of water and allow the rain to come in as well. But we found here another little bark lean-to, and of course stayed there, as we were all tired out, although we had scarcely done ten miles the whole of the day. We soon had a good fire lighted and began our cooking. Bill and I suggested pancakes, so I mixed up a lot of batter in the cups, and, having cut handles for our frying-pans, we began cooking. Now, my notion of a pancake was, and is, that it should be large and thick and puffy, but Bill thought they should be small, thin, and brown. Consequently, when I had my first one well under way, Bill said, 'What do you call *that*?' This was very contemptuously. I was nettled. 'Why, a pancake. What do you call it?' 'Oh, I call it a pudding. You wait till I get my pan fixed, I'll show you what a pancake is.' When he had his first one nearly done, I said, 'Bill, what's *that* you're cooking?' 'Why, a pancake. D—n it, can't you see?' 'That's not a pancake, that's a miserable little hot cake. It's only a wafer.

These are pancakes, Bill; see them, something to eat.' Bill nearly dropped his in the fire. 'Don't you think I know what a pancake is? I've made 'em all over America; and you—why, you're only an Englishman; what do you know, any how?' 'That's your ignorance,' said I; 'I've cooked them in England, in Australia, in the States, and now I'm cooking them on the Selkirk Trail. You're only an American. Why don't you travel and learn something?' Bill got perfectly furious, and if I had chaffed him any more it would have ended in a fight over those miserable cakes. 'Well, well, Bill, call yours pancakes. They are pancakes, Bill; mine are only flapjacks.' Then there was peace in the camp, and the mollified Bill condescended to eat a flapjack and say it was good, while I took one of his, saying it was the best hot cake—no pancake—I had ever eaten.

So we smoked the pipe of peace and lay down, while the rain came through the cracks above us and the melancholy wind howled among the dark and gloomy cedars.

During the night the snow again fell, covering the ground to the depth of four or five inches, and making us as uncomfortable as three poor tramps could be. Still even so, I was, in spite of the pain and inconvenience I suffered, able to observe, in the bright sunshine that happily broke through and mastered the clouds, the beautiful effects of the snow on the near and far landscape. On the long arms of the cedars lay bright patches of snow, and bush and fallen trunks, and jagged stumps, whence the wind had smitten the top of branch and foliage, had their adornment. And in the distance, on the slopes and shoulders of the hills, the snow on the green forest showed thicker and more and more as the eye passed upward, until the green gave way in the overpowering mass of white on the laden limbs, frozen fast in the lofty height, and the snow of the forest joined the snow on the untimbered slopes, running at last into the never-failing frost of the peaks of the range.

It was well I could look at so much, for indeed underfoot things were not so pleasant, and rock and mud and morass made it almost impossible walking; and when, on one occasion, we came to a roaring creek which had to be crossed on a fallen tree, I nearly came to a sudden end of my adventures by slipping on the round wet trunk, although I was fortunate enough to recover my balance. That night we camped again in a cedar forest in a sharp rain, which had come upon us suddenly in the late afternoon.

In the morning, when we came out of our damp shelter into the wet grass and brush, we found that it had ceased raining, though the water still dropped from the heavy branches as they swayed in the wind; and there was some blue sky to be seen among the white clouds above the mountain tops. This day was a repetition of the yesterday, tramping and climbing, getting wet in the brush and drying again in the open, when we came to a clear space below some mountain peak which had been cleared of brush and timber, by a gigantic avalanche or snow slide, from summit to base. Below us at times we could see a confused and hideous pile of jagged tree trunks — fir, pine, cedar, balsam, spruce, and hemlock — piled one above the other, and mixed with rocks and earth, in utter and violent confusion; while, looking up, we could see, too, the ice and snow above the way cleared through the standing forest. My own condition was, of course, no better, for nothing but rest could do my feet any good, and under the circumstances rest was impossible, so I had to plod along, trying to be as Mark Tapleyish as might be, though I confess I doubt even his serenity in such a state of things. But my burden was now growing lighter, for the food was rapidly diminishing, and we knew we could not be very far from the second crossing of the Columbia.

Since we had crossed the Illecilliwet River we had been on its left bank going down; that is, we had been somewhere to the left of it, though how far we did not know. I fancy we were close to it on one occasion, for this day we came to a narrow gorge or cañon, and on crawling to the edge and looking down I saw a furious stream at the bottom two hundred feet beneath me. But we knew that we had to cross this river again before we reached the Columbia, and we speculated anxiously as to how it was to be crossed, whether by raft or swimming, for there was very little likelihood of its being fordable at the second crossing if we could not ford it at the first. But our doubts were solved about noon, when, turning sharply round a turn in the trail, we came upon a broad and rapid stream. We did not know whether this was our river or not, but following the trail for a while we heard the ring of an axe at a little distance. There was evidently somebody thereabouts, and we should be able to make some inquiries. A little farther along the trail we came to a small clearing, and the first logs of a log-cabin. Under a tree was a rude table, made of a slab of split pine, on stakes driven into the ground. There was a log-bench permanently fixed, so that one could sit down. Under another tree was a smouldering fire with a camp oven or skillet, a kettle, and some dirty pans lying in the mud and ashes. Near at hand was a small tent with blankets and a small pile of provisions, flour and biscuit, with some bacon lying on the flour sack. On a big tree close to the trail was this notice:—

'ILLECILLIWET RESTAURANT.
Meals at all hours.'

This was then the Second Crossing, and looking round we could see where the trail ended abruptly in the river.

Presently the sound of the axe ceased, and a man dressed in long boots, blue trousers of dungaree, with a broad-brimmed hat, came out of the forest. He was brown and bearded and unkempt. His hands were brown, hard, and exceedingly dirty, his face the same. We saluted him in a friendly manner, and he gave us separately a 'Morning, pard; on the trail, eh?' Then he asked us whether we wanted meals, stating that his prices were 75 cents a meal; that is, in English money, 3s. 1½d. Fritz and I declined to eat at such terms, but Bill, who had more money than the two of us put together, thought he would have something to eat without cooking it himself, and our new acquaintance prepared him some bacon, boiled some villanous coffee, and heated him up a mass of greasy-looking beans. The bread was certainly solid and satisfying, judging solely from appearances. While the process of preparation was being gone through with deliberation we asked him how we were to get over the river, and were told that he had a boat and would take us across for 50 cents each. In order that we might not attempt to raft it, he gave us an account of how three or four men had fared before he came there. They had, it appears, made a raft on which they put their blankets and saddles, previously making their ponies swim across, and when it was in mid stream the raft capsized. They with difficulty escaped with their lives, and their money, to the amount of about 600 dols., which they had carelessly left in their baggage, was lost.

After Bill had finished eating, we went down to view the boat. This was an extraordinary structure, made of unpainted fir boards an inch thick. It was shaped like a punt, flat bowed and flat sterned, and looked as crazy and cranky a craft as could well be imagined for crossing a rapid and turbulent mountain river. However, there was nothing else for it, and we determined to venture it, bargaining that we were not to pay if we were upset and had to swim for our lives. It was only possible for two at a time to cross, so Fritz and the ferryman went over first. I watched them with a great deal of interest as the river swept them down while they both paddled furiously. But there was no accident. The ferryman hauled his boat up stream along the bank until he got well above where we were on the opposite side, and came across again. Then Bill went over, leaving me till the last. When it came to my turn I could not help thinking of the proverb about the pitcher going often to the well and getting broken at last, considering that the third time might be unlucky. So I took some extra precautions, throwing my coat and long boots off. However, things went very well, and I, too, joined the others, and, having paid my 50 cents, we started off on the last portion of the trail, as we were that evening to come to the Columbia.

Bad as the trail had been before, I think that that last piece of eight or ten miles was really, in many ways, the worst. There was, perhaps, not such hard climbing; it was not so muddy; there were not so many rocks and stones; but the fallen trees lay upon it in numbers innumerable. There would sometimes be two or three close together, and twenty or thirty in a hundred yards. We were crawling over them nearly the whole day, until we were fairly wearied out, and cursed the trees and the whole trail from the bottom of our hearts. But the end of the trail was now nearly at hand. We came at last to where it forked, and on the tree was a notice of some one's ferry over the Columbia, which was declared undeniably the best; on the other hand, there were other notices equally commending another ferry. We took the right-hand fork and went down and down through the forest, on a trail which was now infinitely better and clearer, with ways chopped through the fallen trees. We were in high spirits—that is, the other two were. For my part, nothing but rest could make me 'feel good,' and there was no prospect of that as far as I could see; and I, speaking from experience, defy any one to be happy when there is a goodly portion of skin wanting from his feet, and he has nevertheless to walk, and to walk hard, and to carry a bundle weighing ten or twenty pounds.

But still it was getting towards evening, and a stage in our journey of unknown length was nearly completed, and there would be the respite of camping-time. And presently we saw the forest thinning as the trail descended; in front, above the tree-tops, were other mountains, and soon below we saw the gleam of blue waters and a stretch of sand beyond. We were at the ferry, we paid our money, and in a few moments stood on the other side of the Columbia. Standing silently, I looked back, and between two snow-clad mountains I saw the great gap through which we had toiled. The Columbia was behind us, and the Selkirk Range and the Selkirk Trail

CHAPTER X.

THE GOLDEN RANGE AND THE SHUSHWAP LAKES.

I HAVE seen some rivers in my life in England, in Australia, and in America. There are many most beautiful streams in our own country—the upper Thames with its gentle scenery and placid quietude; the brawling Dove; the splendid Mawddach in Merioneth, between the mountains of Cader Idris and Diphwys; the rapid Eden at Carlisle; and the turbid Severn. In Australia I have seen the bright Murray when it comes from the hills, the sluggish Murrumbidgee, and the Lachlan; in America I have been across the Missouri, the Mississippi, the Brazos, the Colorado, the Ohio, and the Alleghany; but never have I seen a more beautiful and magnificent stream than the Columbia River, at the spot where we had just crossed it. It was bright, blue, deep and calm and strong; not a speck of foam was on its bosom, not a break or a wave marred its mirror, save where a breath of wind touched it lightly as a swallow's wing. Yet it was so strong and earnest, and so bent on doing its work in silence. In the late spring and early summer it is, doubtless, turbid and swollen with the rush of melting snow, but now beauty, majesty, and strength were equally joined—the beauty of the lake with its colour, the majesty of a stream hurrying to the verge of a cataract, the strength of a power that the beaten-down barriers of the mountains had proved.

And before me lay a scene that I felt was worth the toil and pain and endurance that had brought me there to see it. There was no sunlight in the air, for the sky was veiled with a sullen stretch of unbroken cloud, and the air was calm and quiet. Before me was a stretch of white sand and shingle, over which the waters had been running in the spring, and beyond it, on the flat, a few pines and firs lifted their heads above the lower brush, from which rose the blue smoke of some hidden habitations; and far above this the mountains again, opening into three great and gloomy passes, south and west and north. On the loftiest peaks, the sentinels guarding the ways, lay the snow, and low down the bosoms of the hills were the fair garlands of mist and cloud. From the northern pass the river ran, sweeping round the bend to be lost to sight in the southern ways that brought it at last to the Pacific. Through the western pass, a grand and narrow cañon, lay our road over the Golden Range.

We had been speculating all this day as to whether we should be able to get a somewhat civilised meal, for the constant repetition of bacon and bread was beginning to pall upon us. But if we had really hoped for anything we were doomed to disappointment, and all inquiries after a place to get a meal only obtained us the information that we could buy flour and bacon at such and such a canvas tent, which was a store

In making these inquiries I spoke to a pleasant-looking little man, who turned out to be the contractor who had constructed the wagon road through the Eagle Pass, upon which we were to make our way west. He asked me where I was going and offered me work, which I declined, as I wanted to get to the coast. His name was Gus Wright, a man who is very well known in British Columbia. Him I met again in many different places.

As we could not get any one to feed us for love or money, we bought some more bacon and set off down the road in the dark, for it was now late evening, hoping to find a good camping-ground. To make things pleasant for us it began to rain, so that by the time we came to an extremely well-ventilated bark-shelter we were nearly wet through, and by the time we had a fire going we were soaking.

We were camped in a swamp, with a few dead trees around us and a rocky bluff overhead. The wind rose in the night, we heard a tree fall in the gale now and then, and the driving rain came in upon us as we lay, dropping through the miserable roof, and making the ground soft and muddy and our blankets of little avail. In the morning we crawled out before it was dawn and kindled the fire afresh to boil the tea, sitting meanwhile on a log in front of it with our blankets round us, smoking the first pipe.

At noon we came to a camp at a river and got a good meal for 50 cents, and by four o'clock in the afternoon we crossed the Divide after passing three lakes, the last of which was the Summit. At the camp here we had another meal, and walking four miles farther came at dark to the best camping-place we had found yet, as it was absolutely rainproof on the three sides and the roof. Fritz and I were alone by this time, as Bill had insisted on camping at the last lake. Having had dinner so late, or supper so early, we thought it unnecessary to eat again, and devoted our energies to building a glorious fire to dry ourselves and our blankets. We made it of cedar bark, which burns furiously and throws out tremendous heat. We were soon comfortable and slept magnificently. As we made a late start Bill caught us up, and we tramped along as usual. Our objective point was now the Shushwap Lakes, which lay at the end of the road. On these we were told we should find steamers, on which we could get down to the inhabited parts of British Columbia and comparative civilisation. In the Rocky Mountains these steamers had given rise to much discussion, and at first we had thought they ran somewhere down the Columbia to the Arrow Lake, and it was only at the 'Illecilliwet Restaurant' that we had heard positively in what direction we had to go. On leaving Columbia City, or the Second Crossing, we were told the day on which the next steamer was to leave, and now we found we had to make the Lakes this evening, or we should have to wait for the next one. So we pushed on, and it was a terrible day for me. Of course the road was much better than the trail had been, but we made up for that by walking faster, and my feet were getting worse all the while, being so bad at times that I thought I should really be laid up and perhaps entirely incapacitated. We hardly stayed at noon to make tea, and walked along doggedly, without any means of knowing how far we had come, hoping that we should find the distance shorter than we had been told. But it came to night time and a renewal of rain, and still there was no end. We camped at last, for a while, close to the road by a pool of water and ate some supper, and then started out wearily in the dark, without saying anything to each other. It was a case of walking against Time, and I felt sure that he would get the best of us. I began to get tired in addition to the pain, though I said nothing. I could see Fritz on ahead of me, plodding along, and behind me I heard Bill splash, splash through the water on the roads, with an occasional curse as he stumbled against a stone. We were now in a thick dark forest, and began to be a little alarmed, as occasionally I heard noises in the

K

brush which might be caused by bears. Afterwards I found out that they were quite numerous along here. I had no wish to stumble up against one in the dark without any weapon save a knife, so I called to Fritz and asked him if he would camp. No, he was going to the Steamboat Landing. Bill wanted to go on too, so I gave in and we walked another mile. Then Bill called me, and I called Fritz. Bill was going to camp anyhow, so he said, but still Fritz was inexorable, and as I thought that we really could not be far I determined to walk on as well. But after the next hundred yards I began to feel as if it was more than I could do to lift my legs up. My boots seemed as heavy as lead, and my head began to swim, and I almost fell asleep while walking. At last I stopped : 'Fritz, I'm going to camp right here.' 'Very well, I'm going on.' So he left me. But presently I heard him call, and thinking something might have happened I got up, and walking a hundred yards I came to my valiant Teuton, who had 'caved in' at last. He could go no farther, so we cut down a balsam, made a bed, and slept as if we were never going to wake. The bears might have eaten one of us without waking the other, I believe, and it is fortunate they did not try.

In the morning we made breakfast and set out on our last stage, which was about four miles. As we knew we had missed the steamer we did not hurry, and only got to the Landing about two o'clock in the afternoon. We found Bill there, for he had passed us as we slept in the bush without noticing where we lay. By this time he was nearly drunk, as it was possible to get spirits to drink here.

On making inquiries we found that the 'Peerless' steamer would come up next day and leave soon after for the towns of Kamloops and Savona's Ferry, so I had time to look after my miserable feet, which were now in a condition to entitle me to go into a hospital. However, by bathing them and doing nothing, they began to feel a little more comfortable, and the sores dried up and the new skin began to form.

We were not now in a town, or anything resembling one; it was merely a store and whisky saloon, kept by two partners, Murdoch and Hill. Opposite the house, which then consisted of a big bar-room with shelves in it for liquors and dry goods, and a room for eating, was the stable with some hay in it. Besides this there was a log-hut some distance away. This constituted the whole settlement, at that time, of Eagle Pass Landing. It was on the borders of the Great Shushwap (pronounced Su-swop) Lake, which was here nine or ten miles across and surrounded by mountains, which are high enough certainly, but to me looked mere hillocks after the giants of the Rockies and the Selkirks. The Eagle River, which came down the pass we had followed, ran into the lake about a mile from the house, and behind the hill which bounded our view of the lake in front was the Salmon Arm, into which ran the Salmon River. At the junction of the Eagle with the lake waters was another river, of which I knew nothing at this time. It was called the Spallumcheen or Spullamacheen, and came down past an agricultural valley as I was told, though it was hard to believe that there was any land in British Columbia level enough for farming, if I could judge from what I had seen. Behind the house were steep mountains covered with pine, fir, and birch, but there was no snow to be seen.

It was a curious enough sight to sit in Murdoch's and see the little gathering of men there. Murdoch himself was a short, strong-looking man with a good-natured face and agreeable manners, though rather rough, and getting a little grizzled in the beard. Hill, his partner, was a small, boyish-looking fellow, who looked slightly out of place in these wild regions, in a decent suit of black and a good felt hat. Then there was a man named Fairweather, I believe, who talked in a loud and boisterous, bullying tone, as if anxious to make men believe he was a dangerous person, who must be treated with consideration. One or two others, who were waiting, like ourselves, for the boat, completed the company. At times the door would be pushed stealthily open, and an Indian with a soft felt hat over long greasy hair would slide in and show us a pair of well-worn moccasins on flat feet, and ragged trousers and coat to match. He would bring a skin or two—a marten or a beaver or perhaps a fox —and would argue with Murdoch or Hill about the price in a language of which I then knew nothing, and which I supposed to be Indian, but which I afterwards discovered to be Chinook, a barbarous trading jargon made of English, Indian, and French. Then, perhaps, a squaw with her papoose, both a little dirtier than the man, would enter and stare round. They would consult in their own tongue, and then make a bargain or go out without trading, to give way in turn to some other Indians with fish or deermeat.

Altogether I found plenty to amuse me without walking or falling back on my solitary book, 'Sartor Resartus,' and when I got bored or too lazy even to smoke, I retired into a corner and put my head on my blankets and slept for awhile.

In the evening, after supper was over, we gathered round the stove and talked about the railroad, and we who had come from the other side had to give accounts of the progress made there. And then some one from Kamloops or lower down would tell us in return how the road was progressing under Onderdonk, the contractor who had the main British Columbia portion of the C. P. R. under contract. Then would follow yarns and jests, and presently we would pull out the blankets, spread them on the floor where there was least tobacco-juice, and all would be sleeping and snoring.

On the evening of the second day the steamer

came round the point and blew her whistle, which echoed again and again among the mountains, and presently she ran gently on the gravelly beach and let half-a-dozen passengers ashore, who came straight up to Murdoch's. One young fellow rushed in, insisted on standing drinks to the whole crowd, and seizing a box of cigars went round inviting everyone to take a smoke. Meantime I inquired as to when the steamer was to go, and, finding it would not be before morning, I came back to get my share of the fun, if there was to be any. However, there was little, save a few glasses of whisky and a loud gabbling of voices, though some of us amused ourselves by trying to set beaver-traps. These are made of steel, with immensely strong springs, and it is quite a trick to set one. Few can do it without treading on both sides, and it was delightful to see a very light man trying in vain. I could manage it after a few trials. There was only one among us who could set it by hand simply, without treading it, and he was an old trapper. Bear-traps, which are, of course, much more powerful than these, can only be set by using a lever.

In the morning we paid up what we owed, and I got a dollar's worth of bread and deermeat from Murdoch, for my cash was now necessarily getting very low. In fact, when I went on board and paid my seven dollars to go to Savona's Ferry, which was as far as the steamer went, I was again penniless, which seemed then my normal condition. So it was impossible for me to pay fifty cents a meal on the boat and the same for a bed.

The boat was of the usual American shape, with lower and hurricane decks, and was a stern-wheeler, such as, I believe, have lately been introduced in the Nile navigation. She was capable of doing twelve knots or more an hour, and it was certainly necessary that she should be able to make good headway, as the current in the rivers between the lakes is at times tremendous.

We had reckoned on being in Savona's Ferry, about 100 miles away, the next day, but we were doomed to disappointment; for, instead of going direct to Kamloops and then on to Savona, the boat turned to the right instead of the left and picked up a big 'boom of logs,' which she was to tow down to the saw-mill at Kamloops. These were logs cut and thrown into the lakes, and then collected into the boom, which consists of logs connected with a chain, making a ' pen,' as it were, to keep them together. So, instead of going down flying, we had to crawl along, doing about three miles an hour. The scenery was pleasant enough, and at times grand, sometimes heavily timbered and sometimes bare, with the hills terraced as it were. The lake water was deep and dark, and cold to those who were not used to mountain water, but to me it seemed absolutely warm.

When we left the Great Shushwap Lake, and

ran through the connecting river, which was part of the south fork of the Thompson, I had my first view of the Pacific salmon. Standing on the bows, and looking down into the clear, transparent water, I could see hundreds of large fish, from ten to thirty pounds, darting about in every direction. There were fairly tens of thousands of them. At intervals along the banks there were camps of the Shushwap Indians, living in little bark shanties, along the front of which were hung hundreds of split salmon drying in the sun. The little brown children, some of them naked as they were born, would come out and stare at us, and their dogs would yelp and dash a little way into the water. Out in the stream there were a few canoes with a squaw paddling in the stern, while the 'buck' stood up forward with a long spear watching for the passing fish.

My life on board those three days was commonplace and quiet. I slept and smoked and ate my bread and deermeat, and at times talked with some of the deck hands, who were full Indians or half-breeds. Some of the latter were fairly good-looking, and one was positively handsome, while the former were for the most part as ugly as possible.

I read a little, too, in Carlyle, and fancied myself Teufelsdröch on his travels, though mine were certainly of a different character from those celebrated wanderings. And perhaps I borrowed a scrap of a newspaper, which would set me speculating on what the country was like down stream. And sometimes I wondered whether I should get work, and if so what work, and if not what I should do, and so on. Consequently I had no sense of *ennui* on me, and if Fritz or anybody bored me I could easily take refuge in sleep or in the scenery.

So we slowly got down the river, coming more and more into land which looked possible at least for grazing stock, and in places fit for farming, and soon we began to pass stock-farms. We could see bands of cattle and horses, and here and there a house on the river banks, back from which the country now had all along the curious terraced appearance I had noticed occasionally higher up. The timber got less and less, and the appearance of the country was drier. I was told that we had now passed out of the up-country Wet Belt, and were in the Dry Belt, where rain did not fall all the year round.

At last, after a journey which would not have seemed long if I had not known how much faster we might have travelled, had it not been for the logs behind us, we began to come near to Kamloops. I had determined to go no farther than this on the boat, and on representing the matter in the proper light to the captain he returned me the extra fare I had paid to Savona's Ferry. This two dollars was now all my capital.

Late in the evening of the third day, on coming round a bend in the river, we saw the lights of a town and a quarter of an hour after the steamship had blown her whistle we were moored alongside the wharf at the Flour Mill, and taking my blankets on my back I went ashore, after bidding Fritz farewell. I was in Kamloops at last.

CHAPTER XI.

ROUND KAMLOOPS.

AFTER asking where I could find an hotel, I walked from the wharf across a bed of sawdust which was wheeled from the saw-mill adjoining, and came to the street of which Kamloops consists. In a few minutes my blankets were lying on a pile of rugs and valises, and I sat down by the stove to get warm in the bar-room of Ned Cannell, the best known and most popular hotel-keeper in the town. There were fifteen or twenty in the room, most of us smoking or chewing; a few were in the boisterous stage of incipient intoxication, and some two or three were lying helplessly on the floor. I could hear snatches of conversation. 'Come, step us, boys, what's your liquor?' 'Take a smile;' 'Oh now, don't give us taffy;' 'What's this you're telling me?' or, 'Say, Jack, got a chew o' terbacker? hand us your plug.' Then there was talk of the railroad, which, of course, was the all-absorbing topic, some prophesying prosperity, and some universal ruin and desolation as its result. 'See now, pard, Montána was a good country before the Northern Pacific was put through, and what is it now? Why, a few years ago cow-boys were getting 45 and 50 dols. a month, and now wages is down to 25 or 30.' Everybody judged solely from his own experience, as men mostly do in matters which affect the pocket.

I found there was no work to be done except railroad work, and of that I had had a sickener, and when I found that white men's wages here were only 1·75 dol. for such work, and that there were hordes of Chinamen introduced into the country to compete with our race, I began to think I had come to a curious country. But I lay back taking it as easy as possible, and, under the narcotic influence of much nicotine, sank into a lethargic state of indifference; in fact, I chewed myself into a state of coma, like Dickens's Elijah Pogram. About a quarter to twelve some of the company began to go, and, as all the beds in the house were full, about a dozen of us slept in our blankets all about the bar-room, and in an alcove where stood a diminutive billiard-table.

In the morning I was out early and took a look at the town. It consisted then of a long straight street of wooden houses, some of them quite handsome structures, especially when I compared them with the log-shacks I had been living in. This street, on both sides of which were houses, runs at some little elevation above the river, which is here the Thompson, with its fall waters, as the South Fork down which I had come the day before, is joined by the North Fork, the junction taking place right in front of the town. Across the river, in the corner of land washed by the two rivers, was the Reservation for the Kamloops Indians, with their dirty little town of miserable huts, and behind this a steep, barren, and treeless mountain, which had the peculiarity to me of always looking as if it was partly in shade and partly in light, owing to the difference in colours of the mass. In fact, it gave me somewhat the same impression, in that respect, as St. Paul's in London does when one sees the clean and discoloured portions of the stones in contrast.

On the opposite side of the South Fork was a stretch of flat country running gradually up in the background to hill and mountains and a confusion of peaks. These mountains are but sparsely wooded in comparison with the ranges in the upper country.

My object was now to get work if I could, so I went to the saw-mill and the flour-mill, but was unsuccessful there, and I found nothing in the rest of the town. When I was thoroughly satisfied that it was useless to trouble myself any more in this place, I met Bill, who was in an advanced state of intoxication. He rushed out of Edward's hotel, clawed hold of me to keep himself up, saying, 'Come and have a drink, Texas?' I would much rather have left it and him alone, but there was no denying him, and I had to take something. Then it was, 'Take another,' but I refused firmly.

'Well, anyhow, you'll come and have dinner with me, Texas; I know you can't have much money.' Now this was very kind, and I did have dinner with him, though he worried me all the time by behaving as if he was in camp under a cedar, glaring round wildly, clawing at things unsteadily, and capsizing his tea on the table. Still, it is nothing uncommon in that country for a few men at table to be drunk, and nobody marks them if they are not quarrelsome.

After dinner I thought it was time to get out of town. It was no use staying there with 1 dol., which was now all I had, and I thought there might be a chance of getting work in the country, as I was told that there were many cattle ranches in this part of British Columbia. So I slung my blankets on my back and set off, consoling myself with the thought that, if I was unsuccessful, at any rate I was going west, and might reckon on reaching the Pacific in time if I did not starve on the way. I set off on the road which led to Savona Ferry, and walked steadily in spite of my feet, which soon began to hurt me again, although they had been better during the last few days of comparative rest. For three miles or so my way lay uphill through a dry, barren-looking country, with here and there the efflorescence of alkali showing among the coarse grass and whitening the baked mud at the bottom of the dried water-holes. The trees were bull-pines with red scaly trunks of a foot or two in diameter for the most part, with here and there a fir, or occasionally a tree that looked like a dwarf cotton-wood. Here and there were a few horses, that lifted their heads to look at me, and then went on grazing assiduously. Then I would come upon a band of cattle. These would start a little, then run into a cluster, and stand staring with the boldest in front, perhaps pawing the dusty ground or bellowing. They would stand so until I got out of sight, and then some would come to the next rise to have another look at my departing figure. Four miles from town I came to a woodcutters' camp, and stayed awhile to talk with the one man in camp, who was from Missouri, but had not been there for twenty years. From him I learnt there was a ranche about seven or eight miles farther on, and I bade him farewell and tramped along, making nearly four miles an hour. As I came round a curve in the road, past a dried alkali lake which was white as snow, I saw a little house on a rise with farm buildings near at hand, and on the side nearest to me a man was working with two horses, driving them round and round in a ring, while he stood in the middle holding the reins, or lines as they call them in America. There was a woman with him who was using a hay fork. On coming closer I found they were thrashing out grain in this primitive manner, something in the way they must have done in the ancient days spoken of in the Old Testament, when it was forbidden to muzzle the oxen that tread out the corn. I climbed over the fence and went down towards them. As I came up the man stopped his horses. He was a hard, wiry-looking individual, with keen eyes, scanty beard and moustache, weather-beaten skin, a good mouth and teeth. He wore long boots, into which an ancient pair of blue trousers were tucked, a waistcoat unbuttoned showing a white shirt, and no coat. His hands were hard and muscular, with the glazed appearance on the backs one so often sees in old seamen. In spite of this rig-out, I saw at once he was not an ordinary British Columbian, but was probably an educated man, and possibly an Englishman. I was more puzzled by the woman, who was an Indian I could see, short and strong-looking, with strongly-marked features, and such a look of intelligence and such a smile on her face that I almost doubted my first impression as to her race. I spoke to him, 'Good afternoon, sir; are you the boss here?' He smiled: 'Well, I guess I am, unless she is,' he said, pointing to the woman, who grinned, and then laughed genially, but said nothing. 'You're an Englishman?' I confessed to my nationality, and he said, 'So am I. Are you travelling?' I explained that I was looking for work, and asked if he could help me to get any. 'I'm too poor to hire anyone just now, and I must get on as I can by myself,' said he, 'but you can go up to the house if you would like a cup of tea; my wife will give you some.' I thanked him and went up to the house, and sat down in the kitchen, where I was soon drinking tea and eating corned beef. Presently my host came up and sat down to talk. He told me that his name was Hughes, that he was an Englishman, that he had been a sailor in the East India trade, had left the company and taken to running opium into China. After this he came to California soon after the days of '49, and mined for fourteen years in that State without much success, and since that time he had been in British Columbia working for Gus Wright, the man I had met up at the second crossing of the Columbia, and mining on his own account, and that now he was in the cattle-raising business. In return for this confidence I told him my history, how I had been in Australia and at sea, speaking of my life in London and my adventures since then. Finally, it grew so late while we were talking, that he asked me to stay there all night and make a fresh start in the morning.

That evening, after supper, we had a long talk about things in general—about emigration, about English politics, in which he still took an interest, being an ardent Conservative. This is, I find, very often the case with Englishmen living abroad, though I found their adherence to Conservatism was, for the most part, based on the belief that that party is the most consistent in foreign politics and pledged to an Imperial policy. On the other hand, the Liberalism which would allow the Colonies to go their own way is thought contemptible and narrow-minded and

L

selfish. I may take this opportunity of saying that I have found the Colonies generally more devoted to the mother country than she generally is to them, although the affection of the human parent for the child is, as a rule, greater than that of child for parent.

From politics we ran into philosophy and religion, and we chatted for hours on agnosticism and atheism, on religion as it is and as it should be, and diverged into literature. I found him a very well-informed man, considering everything, and by no means bigoted.

He told me, however, in confidence that he was not beloved by his neighbours, and I found this to be true; but, considering their general ignorance, that was a compliment to him.

Before going to bed he told me that I might possibly find work at the next ranche, belonging to a Mr. Roper, who was a good boss, he said. If I was unsuccessful there I could go over to the Lake, about three miles from Roper's, to where the railroad was being made, and try there. Finally, if I was unsuccessful at both places, I might come back to him, and he would give me a week or two's work at a dollar a day. So I thanked him, and went to sleep on a pile of rugs in the corner of the room.

In the morning I had breakfast, shook hands with him, in case I should not come back, and set off down the road. I found Mr. Roper, but could get no work there, so I went over to Ferguson's on the Lake, where two tunnels were being made.

I found Mr. Ferguson, but he, too, had no work for me unless I could drill. As I was unable to tackle this job on account of ignorance, I walked down the grade, finding large gangs of Chinamen at work at different places, in charge of a white man, who was called the 'herder.' This job is not always a happy one, although it is well paid, for the Chinamen who work on railroads are the very scum of China, 'wharf rats' from Hong Kong, and are evil and desperate. Consequently it is no uncommon thing for a 'herder' to get killed or badly beaten by them if anything goes wrong, and sometimes in protecting himself he will have to shoot several of them when they run at him with picks and shovels.

After walking some distance I came to the boss of part of the work, who gave me directions how to get back to Hughes's Ranche without retracing my steps. I had to climb up a terribly steep hill, and then walk two or three miles through open timber, finally coming out just at the spot I had aimed at. I went down to the ranche and shook hands with Hughes. That evening I bathed my feet, which had broken out again in sores and blisters, and Mrs. Hughes gave me a pair of buckskin moccasins, in which it was a perfect delight to walk after going about in my big boots. I stayed at this ranche two weeks, and was kindly treated in every way. We had good food and plenty of it, and did not work long hours. I gathered rocks for a stone wall and drove a scraper team to fill up holes round the near farm buildings. Sometimes I dug potatoes or gathered beans, and at night we had long conversations about all possible things, or I read the English illustrated papers or wrote letters. My health here was better than it had been at any time since I had left home, for the air was magnificent. The scenery was not grand, but beautiful and quiet. Below the house was a stretch of flat meadow, beyond it birch and cottonwood, over these ranges of grass with a few bull pines, and above and beyond these the spurs of the range which divided us from the Nicola Valley.

At last one night Hughes told me that he had no more need of help, and that we must part on the morrow. I was more than sorry to go, but at any rate this comparative rest had done me much good. My feet were thoroughly healed and I had fifteen dollars in my pocket. In the morning I set out alone, this time determined not to stop or stay until I reached the coast. I promised to write to Hughes and he promised to answer.

That evening I reached Savona's Ferry at the west end of Kamloops Lake, and stayed in a hotel kept by Adam Ferguson, one of the handsomest men I ever saw in British Columbia.

I was now in the Alkali Dry Belt, where the rain is very scanty and the ground brown and the grass parched and burnt. The water is often very bad and unfit for drinking. My next day's solitary walk was over a high, almost level plain, on a good road with a few climbs, when it plunged into a cañon and came up again on the other side. The scenery was desolate but beautiful, the hills were rounded but in the distance lofty, and here and there the country was cut up into mounds or buttes and bluffs, with now and again terrace rising above terrace. The hillsides were cut sometimes like irregular channelling in an Ionic column, and the few trees gave the place a more solitary look than if it had been bare. As I had crossed the Thompson River at Savona it was now on my left hand, and it ran turbulently over rock and rapid far below me, in its calmer intervals bright and blue, while the noise of the rapids was like the roar of the breakers when one hears them from a long distance. At times the winding road took me far from the river back towards the hills, and sometimes I was in the middle of a plain, the only sign of life in it. I had dinner at the Eight Mile House, so called on the *lucus a non lucendo* principle, for it was thirteen miles from Savona and twelve from Cache Creek. Here I found three teamsters at dinner, who were bound the same way as myself, with empty wagons. I remember one went by the extraordinary nickname of 'Hog Hollow Bill,' which I found out afterwards was given him because he came from a place of that name in Missouri. I started to walk before they had their teams hitched up. While I was getting ready to go the woman who kept the house went outside to see one of the men tie a kettle to the tail of an unfortunate cur who had made his home there. Her child began to cry aloud about something, and she ran in, caught it up, saying: 'There, duckie, don't cry; come and see Jim tie a kettle to the doggie's tail.' I was happy to see that the instrument of torture parted company with the dog after the first hundred yards, while this mother was giving her child a first lesson in cruelty to animals. After walking a mile the wagons caught me up, and I was invited to take a ride on one of them, and by this means I got into Cache Creek before dark. This place consists of two or three houses, a hotel, a store, and an express office. The Buonaparte Creek comes down this way, and it is here that the wagon-road turns off to Cariboo, the great mining-place in British Columbia. I got vile food and viler accommodation, and all the bar-room talk was about the extortionate charges on the railroad. They told me about a horse, which was worth 40 dols., for which the owner was asked 75 dols. for transportation. He told the railroad men to keep the horse.

In the morning I continued the journey on the wagon with my friendly teamster, and after going through much the same country came at noon to 'Oregon Jack's.' Oregon Jack had been in British Columbia more than twenty years, and had never been sober since he entered the country. It is not known how many years he had been drunk in Oregon, but testimony from all sides averred that his intoxication had been constant on the north side of the 49th parallel. He was a little bald-headed man, with red face and leering, satyr-like eyes, and he certainly was drunk when I saw him, though able to talk fluently about being perfectly sober, 'though I was drunk when you were last here, Bill.'

We afterwards passed Cornwall's, the hotel kept by the Governor of British Columbia. This was the quietest, most comfortable hotel on the road, with lots of English papers lying round the rooms. In the evening we came to Eighty-nine—that is, eighty-nine miles from Yale, and stayed at French Pete's. There were a dozen wagons here, going up and down, and the teamsters made things so lively that soon after supper, which was cooked by French Pete's Indian wife, I took my blankets outside and got into my teamster's wagon and slept there comfortably, although it was a rather frosty night. The hills on both sides of the river were now drawing closer together and the character of the country was changing, as if we were approaching mountains again. I asked the teamster about this, and he said I was coming now to the Cascade Range, and that I should enter the cañon at Cook's Ferry. Accordingly a little afterwards I began to see larger hills and mountains, while the river ran more rapidly over rocks, breaking in foam down long rapids, and when unbroken running round the bends with a quiet velocity even more impressive than the noisy rush of the broken waters.

Soon after noon we crossed the bridge at the ferry and passed to the left side of the stream. This was the end of the track in this direction.

Since leaving the summit of the Rocky Mountains, where I had last heard the whistle of the eastern locomotives, I had traversed mountains, lakes, and plains on foot, by steamer, and by wagon, and had come 360 miles to hear them again. And I had yet 180 miles to pass before I should reach the coast.

CHAPTER XII.

THROUGH THE FRASER CAÑON.

I HAD, up to the moment of my leaving Cook's Ferry, deluded myself with the thought that I was coming at last to some beautiful evidences of civilisation. After passing each comfortable ranche and seeing the prosperity of fat cattle and plentiful horses, I said to myself, 'I shall soon be in El Dorado, where, perhaps, there is a library with books to be read; perhaps there may be men who are civilised and educated, even so far the delightful victims of our pleasures as to be acquainted with chess. Then, instead of playing draughts on a tree stump, rudely marked out with a burnt stick, in the primæval forest, I may sit by a fire, with a cup of coffee near at hand and a pipe of good tobacco, and astonish my opponent with a crafty Muzio or a well-played Evans. Or I may play mild bumblepuppy, or even whist, instead of fierce poker, or insidious euchre or assassinating cut-throat.' But now it seemed that my airy visions and dream castles were to be shocked and shaken down. My library of books eager to be read, my chess-table with opponent waiting, my smoking cup of coffee, vanished from my imagination when once more a tremendous barrier of rock and mountain, thrust high into the black clouds above, came before me and shut me for a time, unmeasurable until passed through, from level land, if such there were, and from coast and Pacific, whose imagined roar was driven from my ears by sound of wind and river.

For the Cascades were in front of me, frowning, and the Thompson ran mockingly past, while I toiled slowly up the road into the labyrinth of hills.

And yet I was light-hearted, for my feet were whole and sound, and I heard again in my pocket the jingle of pleasant silver. The road, if steep at times, was at any rate well made, and the change from the cloudless blue of the Dry Belt to the broken harmony of cloud and clear sky, mist and rain, and green of tree or grass, was sweet. So as I climbed I watched the fretting river that had worn its way through these hills for thousands of years—for a geologic age perchance, and when I rested I sat on a fallen tree under which, when in its first youth and glory, perhaps the pioneer Indian who found the pass had come, and upon whose fallen trunk had rested, it might also be, the most adventurous of the white trappers when the Hudson Bay Company were sovereign in these solitudes. And when I wandered from the road and sat down by the river, or lay by a little brawling creek to rest, I was, as it were, the first myself in this realm of nature. The white trapper was yet unborn in the home of his fathers, and the Indian a little farther yet in the unknown, while his tribe are on the plains of the east or among the timber of the coast. Or the abode of his fathers is farther yet, even beyond Alaska—yea, even beyond Behring's Straits, in the mystic land of Asia, mother of nations, fertile and not yet past childbearing, though a Sarah among the younger lands.

But no! am I dreaming or awake? For there is my Indian coming down the pass; verily an Indian, and a dirty one, with his long greasy locks and the moccasins. This is no pioneer. No; but here is the white man's pioneer. I hear a shriek and a rush and a roar, and as I look up, staring across the foam to yon shelf of rock, on it there sweeps, like an embodied hurricane, the Engine and the Train, the Power and the Deed. And my pioneer of Indians looks not up; his thoughts are far away, perhaps to the times before the white man was; or, perhaps, they are but dreams stomachic as to where the next dinner may be begged. For so has the Indian fallen!

> Have the elder races halted?
> Do they droop and end their lesson . . .
> We take up the task eternal, and the burden and the lesson,
> Pioneers! O Pioneers!

So went that day's walk in the cañon or valley of the Thompson, so soon to lose its name and be mingled with the waters of the greater and longer river the Fraser. And as the evening came on the sky got sullen and drooped wearily, until it rested on the mountains, and a chill, sharp wind came from the gorges, keen and hard and piercing, like the ranked spear points of an invisible host or close flight of unseen magic arrows. And I walked quicker and quicker, for I was but thinly clad—nay, almost unclad against such ice breezes from the north, and still in solitude. But I came round a corner and saw four Indians—two women, one old and one young, and two children, a boy and a girl. The older woman was of any age, but surely nearly ready for her rest in those quaint fantastic graveyards in which the Indians put their dead, adorning the guardian railing with globes, spikes and strange painted figures of carven cocks, and figure dummies on the graves under tents, to keep off the snow and hail and biting wind. Yet she was heavily burdened with a large roll of blankets or rugs, in the middle of which was perhaps a package of evilly smelling salmon, supported by a broad pack-strap on her forehead. And the poor little children were bearing packs bigger than themselves. It was happy that the wind was behind them, or how else could they toil up that slope, although so much better a road than their old ancient trail, which at times came in sight as the white man's broad way crossed and supplanted it, leaving the briers and brush and weeds to encumber and choke it up? The old woman greeted me: 'Clahya.' 'Clahya,' said I, and passed on, melancholy for myself, but sadder yet for them.

And yet another step, and I see the earliest lights of Lytton stretched along a little flat; I see the Fraser, turbid and swollen, bursting from its northern hills; and I see the Thompson's blue beauty overpowered in the whitened stream, like a bluebell smitten by discoloured snow. But still it shows, as might a petal, along the nearer shore a thin, diminishing band of light amethyst against the broad colour of grey jade.

And now I come down to men's habitations, where Indians and whites dwell together. I walked into the bar-room of Bailey's Hotel and found my white host as drunk as an Indian might be, yet good-tempered and smiling and amorous of his fiddle, which he embraced lovingly. It was there I stayed that night, amid some noise and disorder, while outside the rain and sleet drove down from the hills.

In the early morning, after breakfast, I set out again on another solitary stage; and now the Jackass Mountain was to be climbed. I know not why Jackass, unless it be that none but a jackass could or would climb it. Be that as it may, it was a long and steady pull against that height, and I was tired and nigh breathless when I paused on the summit, where a bridge hung against the wall of rock above, and I could look down eleven hundred feet of almost sheer depth to the Fraser that was silent beneath me! The rain had ceased in the morning, but the air was damp and chill. The clouds capped the pine-clad heights and drooped in long streamers down the slopes, touching bold rock and precipice into faint mystery, and leaving dew or unshed rain on fir and pine. The swift river crawled slowly below, like a train that seems to fly when we are in it and to lag dismally in the far background, and its roar was hidden in the faint murmur of the wind or the startling chirp of bird or squirrel. And even now, as I write, from that bridge could one see the river, for it crawls by as it has crawled for ages that are an eternity to us. And I saw it for an unspeakable moment, and passed down the steep and precipitous road, above whose verge trees that sprang from roots clutched round rocks two hundred feet below showed their slender waving crowns and spire of branches.

From my mind now all trace of the picturing vision of the day or two ago had passed, and books, or chess, or men of converse were far removed from my mind; and yet the vision had been no deceitful one, nor had a lying spirit lied to me. I was nearer to civilisation, to a pioneer camp of civilisation than I knew, and the next house was the spot I should have dreamed of. I came to it. It had all the semblance of a hotel—verandah and benches outside, big front door to let the weary or thirsty traveller in or to drag the intoxicated one out for refreshment and sobering. I went up, took hold of the handle, muttering to myself, 'It is surely dinner time. I smell something.' Had I been he who said, ' Fee-fo-fum,' I should have smelt the blood of an Englishman.

The handle turned but the door was locked. It was strange but explicable. Perhaps every one inside was asleep—and drunk. Perhaps they had stayed up till morning playing poker, and were tired. So round I went to the back door. Yes, there was somebody there; for dinners don't cook themselves, except as in Lamb's story of Roast Pig, and this savour in the air was not porcine. Another step brought me to the door. I peeped in, and fell back more than surprised. I was surely dreaming. I looked again. I saw an individual in a cassock—long and black! He turned and saw me. What he saw I know not exactly—a tall ruffian, with red curly beard, long moustache, brown hair, long and nearly to his shoulders, brown eyes, and a big broad-brimmed hat, my dear old Texas hat, now much ventilated with holes, and blue trousers tucked, of course, into long and muddy boots. I saw a pleasant, bright, youthful and intelligent English face, and when he spoke I heard my mother tongue spoken as it should be spoken, in a manner which it seemed to me I must have forgotten, for it sounded so strange.

'Good morning, sir. Can I get dinner here?' said I. 'Come in,' said he, 'and I will ask Mr. S——.' I went in, and he led me to what had been the bar-room in this old hotel, for such it had been.

Heavens! what an alteration from the days when men lounged and drank and spat here! For whisky and liquor shelves, books and a bookcase; for hacked benches, comfortable lounging-chairs; for floor adornment of saliva and discarded chews and old cigar stumps, neat carpets; and instead of smoke reek and brandy fume, odour of calf and morocco and vellum! I sat down stunned and astonished, not able yet to realise what I looked like in such a place, else should I have disappeared through the window, or put my bull head through the panel of the door, and gone off, like Samson bearing the gates of Gaza, a giant through fright. The opposite door opened and another cassock appeared—another mage. But he spoke in a pleasant voice and held out his hand, and when he learnt what I wanted, which at first I had forgotten, having to fish round for my stray intention in my surprised, dislocated mind, asked me cordially to join them at dinner if I would excuse the rough fare, which, he said, could not be much in such a desolate place.

Fare! why what was fare to me if I was to dine with two magicians, two wizards, with, by-the-by, a third in training? For there was a bright young boy face to be seen too, and another gentle voice. Would not a Barmecide feast satisfy? for then I could talk the freelier, and interchange mind with mind, and be, perhaps, witty or humorous or pathetic, though, Heaven knows, I was a pathetic figure enough to those with eyes to see and hearts to know.

So we sat down to dinner—salmon, bread, potatoes, with pie to follow.

We talked.

'Have you come down from the upper country or are you going up towards Kamloops?' asked the elder magician, clean shaven and healthy and bright-eyed.

'I'm just tramping down from near Kamloops, where I was working,' said I, 'and I'm bound for the coast, to see what can be done down there.'

'How did you like Kamloops?'

'Not much. Too much drunkenness and fighting. I am rough myself, as you see, but I like quietness and order.' This was a little hypocrisy.

'You are an Englishman, are you not?' said the younger clergyman.

'I am; everybody finds that out. So are you, both of you. Is it not so?'

'Yes, we are both from the old country.'

'Well, it is an extraordinary place to find two clergymen in. I must own I was so surprised that I felt as if I was dreaming. I thought I was coming to an ordinary hotel, and then to see you here!'

'That is nothing; very often men come along and insist this is an hotel. Of course it used to be one. Won't you take some pie?'

'Thank you,' and a piece of very suspicious-looking paste was put on my plate.

The younger man, whose name I found was

M

Edwards, looked very doubtfully at it as he gave it to me, and said, 'I made that.'

'Indeed; then it must be good,' said I, courteously.

'Oh no; I never made one before in my life, and the paste seems so hard, and unlike pies that other people make.'

I tasted it, and it was like a board, solid, unbendable, durable, and waterproof. 'Pray, sir, how did you make it?'

'Just of flour and water.'

'What, no grease or baking soda?'

'Not a bit.'

I broke into a peal of laughter. They were so kind and sociable that I was now at my ease. 'Then it is certainly a new kind of pie.'

Mr. Edwards looked very rueful. 'Well, I'm sure I never thought it was so hard to cook. There's some flour and water mixed up now in the kitchen, and it won't stick together, but lies in flakes, however much I knead it.'

I burst out again into a very broad smile. 'Put more water in, sir, and see if that will do any good.'

'Well, Mr. ——, I wish you had come along a little earlier, and your advice and assistance would have given us a better dinner.'

'A better dinner I don't want. It is far more pleasure to me to talk to two of my countrymen, who are educated, than to eat a dinner that would suit a *gourmet.*'

'Well, then, let us go into the book-room and have a smoke.'

In the library they gave me some good English cigarettes, and we all sat down. But it was impossible for me to be there and not examine the shelves.

'Pray, sir,' said I, 'may I look at your books?' and without waiting for permission, so eager was I, went to the opposite shelves. They were rather disappointing, however, there, being mostly theological. I ran my fingers along the shelf: Eusebius, Mosheim, Milman, Paley, Butler—familiar enough names, but not in my line at all. When I came to Eusebius I read the name out.

'Do you know him?' asked Mr. Small, smiling, thinking, doubtless, he was a name only.

'Why, no, I don't know him, but I've seen him quoted in Gibbon's "Decline and Fall."'

'Oh, indeed, have you read that?'

'Yes, sir, I read it first before I was twelve, and once since then.'

Then to another shelf. Poets here: Shakspere, Keats, but no Shelley—too much of an atheist, may be, I thought—and various others. And then the classics —Horace, Virgil and a huge Corpus Latinorum, and another of the Greek poets and tragedians. I came to Catullus. 'I think Catullus is my favourite, sir, among the Romans. What do you think?'

'Well, I am rather surprised. Can you read Latin?'

'A little. I learnt some, and I have managed not to wholly forget it, like most when they leave school or college.'

'Then were you at college?'

'Not at Oxford or Cambridge; though I know both well. You are of one of these universities?'

'Oxford,' said Mr. Small.

'And you, sir?' said I, turning to the other.

'Only from Durham.'

Then I sat down again, and we had a long and delightful conversation. Mr. Small showed me a beautiful edition of Horace published by Bell and Daldy, illustrated with cuts from coins and medals. He read an ode or two, the 'Fons Bandusiæ, splendidior vitro,' and 'Persicos odi apparatus,' and I read Catullus's 'Lugete, Veneres Cupidinesque,' the most wholly delightful piece of poetry in the whole range of Latin literature; and finally, getting more enthusiastic, we came to Greek, and Mr. Small read from some of the plays of the dramatists, kindly keeping to those I knew, for my knowledge of Greek was always small, and confined to the dramatists and a little Homer. In fact, I ground my way through Sophocles, Æschylus, and some of Euripides with aid of translations, solely for the sake of the poetry.

Then we ran on into English, and talked for hours of the poets, until it began to grow dark and the wind howled and a little rain fell, and it was time for me to go, before the fiercer rain began. So I shook hands with both my friends and the younger boy and set out, as they wished me 'God-speed' and turned back into the lighted room. And I was in mud and water and forest and mountain, and the shades of Greek and Roman flew before the blast like dried leaves from the tree of knowledge.

These two gentlemen were High Church English clergymen, who had come out there as missionaries for the Indians. What a terrible sacrifice to make! It seems to me waste of such lives; but yet what goodness of heart and strength of conviction must have led these to leave a land of culture and expatriate themselves among these mountains, and men ruder than the mountains!

So I thought as I walked along, splashing in the pools made by the rain that had fallen as we had been talking. And as it grew dark I came to some houses. I knocked at the door of one, and was answered in Chinook by a slattern of an Indian woman whom I could see through a crack in the door. I insisted on English, and finally got out of her that there was a hotel farther on. Another mile of tramping and another house. I tried again and found this full of Indians and half-breeds, who told me to go farther yet. Finally I came to the hotel, after two more miles of tramp in bright moonlight, for the clouds had passed away. And the moon above me threw such strong shadows of blackness under brush and tree, and such silver floods on the open ground, that the alternation of light and shade gave the appearance of snow.

I stamped into the usual bar-room, greeted the owner of the hotel and store, nodded to a man by the stove, said 'Clahya' to an Indian woman with a baby, and sat down to smoke and dry myself.

And in the morning, clear and fresh, but threatening rain, the road lay before me again. Again miles of solitary walking towards the Elysium that lies beyond the rainbow. At noon I came to Boston Bar, the commencement of the wildest and most terrible part of the Fraser Cañon, where the mountain bases lie close and closer together, and the fierce flood of water boils and surges through its deep and narrow chasm, until it breaks its bonds and frees itself at Yale. This Boston Bar is named from the bar of sand and shingle in the river, which was in early days a great mining place, and is even yet worked at times by Chinamen. Just below the Bar is the sullen-looking gorge, fringed with clouds, into which road and river run. And this was my way.

This cañon is other than the cañons, passes, and gorges in the Rockies and Selkirks. All are narrow and mountainous, heavily clad with timber, but there is something about this that makes it stranger and wilder and sterner. It may perhaps seem so in my mind, because the days I passed in it were cloudy and sullen, with every now and then a gust of wind and an hour of rain, for it was then nearing winter, and though the snow lay not yet upon the mountains, the air was shrewd and bitter. But the main feature which influenced my mind was the steepness of the lofty precipices, from whose heights fall after fall, cascade after cascade, leapt to the valley a thousand feet at a bound, swayed by the wind like silver ribbons, or dissipated into foam and spray. And here I noticed how strangely slow the water of a lofty fall appears to come down. There is no swift plunge of mighty waters such as Niagara's, but the slow dropping of the thin light line of the mountain stream, running through a fringe of misty cloud that hangs upon the breast of the hills.

And all along the road were evidences of the Indians. In the trees were boxes built to keep dried salmon in, secure from thieves and prowling beasts, and here and there were slender stages built out over the terrible stream, on which the Indians stand when the salmon come up the river, holding a net like a magnified racquet-bat, in which they catch the fish as they pass. Graveyards too there were at intervals, each stranger than the last. And I came at evening with a new companion, the man who was at the hotel with me the night before, to another little wayside inn, kept by a Portuguese from the Azores, who gave us the best meal that I had eaten for many a long day. It was necessary, for that fatal pie had given me a terrible attack of indigestion, which lasted three days.

I spent a pleasant evening in that little house in the lonely cañon, while outside the river chafed and roared, and the river of wind over it swept down between the hills, eddying and swirling over the trees, as the rain pattered ceaselessly on the roof, gathering in pools on the road, and running down to add to the turbid volume of the Fraser.

It was nearly noon next day before we started, and then it was made in desperation of its clearing up. But, as if to cheer us for our courage, the clouds drifted away before a cold north wind and the rain ceased. So we came to Hell Gate dry, and could stand with some patience for a while to see the river roar through the pass of ill-omened name.

Here the river ran at its narrowest, and here it must have been the deepest. The huge rocks jutted out on each side into the boiling current, and were bare and black-looking. The river looked strange and dangerous, alive and struggling like a python in the toils, and at times ran backwards on the surface, while below it was fiercer still, finding its destined way down through cavern and bar, and leaping at last to the surface to roar above the level of the main stream, curling and coiling and eddying in confusion worse confounded. Here at flood-time, after snow-melting in the distant northern home of that river and in the Golden Range, source of the Eagle, and the lakes whence come the Thompson, its tributary, the waters rise in revolt and despair, and storm this Bastille Gate of Rocks, climbing higher and higher, roaring louder and louder still, whirling pine and fir trunks down like straws, to suck them under in a maëlstrom that makes the quick eye giddy, finally lifting its foaming crest above the barrier, to scream like a freed eagle and leap rejoicing down the wider ways. And when it passes and the floods are over, where is the road? Washed into the stream, and the bare rock is left. See, as we stand here, on the road high above our heads is a red line painted on the rocks. So high can this river rise, and it may be higher yet.

So, after watching the Gate for an hour, we passed on and found a bridge below, and crossed thereon to the right bank. Surely we were nearly to Yale. But it seemed impossible. How could a town be put into this cañon? The shelf of rock on which the trains ran in such seeming peril above the terrible waters had been cut and carved out by huge labour of years. Was it possible a town could be near? It was possible truly, and we were close to it when we turned and saw a vast pool of quiet water, with a long eddy that took a floating log round and round for an hour as we sat smoking in quiet, never letting it approach the verge of the lower rapid. Round this pool were tremendous mountains steep and sheer, but across the water, on a little flat, was a house right under the hills, and on the sand an Indian canoe. On the highest crests of the hills the hand of winter had been laid, for there was a gleam of scanty snow, and save that house which sent up no smoke as sign of habitation, making the scene thus even more desolate than snow and sullen mountain could by themselves, there was no appearance of life.

So we rose and took up our blankets, and a hundred yards farther on we came round a corner, and Yale was before us, snugly settled down on a little flat space at the foot of the hills, smoking from many chimneys, while on the beach under the town lay a steamer. We were then on navigable waters. We and the Fraser were free of the hills. I turned, looked up the cañon, frowning and stupendous, and walked into the town.

CHAPTER XIII.

DOWN STREAM TO THE COAST.

THAT night I and my partner, who was a little insignificant chap, 'a man of no account,' slept and ate at the nearest hotel, a very refuge for tramps, undelightful, dirty, with bad cooking and worse beds. Kept by a semi-intoxicated, wholly disreputable landlord, who kept on giving me good advice with regard to my morality, which, he feared, would be undermined by the license and drunkenness among whites and Indian 'klootchmen,' or women on the coast, it was the haunt and rendezvous for undelectable characters from the other parts of the town. We were first amused by two or three of the Yale *demi-monde*, who came to Taylor's to get more drink, being at that time rather more merry than wise, and the more drink resulted in a quaint fandango, or semi-cancan, danced, on the floor first and then on the counter, by a bright little dark-eyed Mexican girl, with brilliant teeth and coils of hair and a strange dress of purple and reddish colours interwoven, who, as she danced, sang snatches of Spanish songs and

English too, every now and again cursing volubly in both. And late at night there was a ferocious encounter of tongues between our host and his housekeeper, a voluble, vicious, snap-eyed woman, who stuck out her chin and placed her arms a-kimbo, the cause of dispute being Taylor's half-bred Indian child, which this virtuous woman, 'far above rubies,' declined to wash or otherwise tend on account of the luckless infant's illegitimacy. Result: furious war of tongues, and at times I feared a personal encounter. Both appealed to me. 'Should I wash a dirty little Indian bastard, sir?' says she. 'Don't you think she should, sir?' says Taylor plaintively, but getting fierce again when talking to her. The end of it was banging of doors and screaming inside, while Taylor himself and an old white-haired Mexican took charge of the little girl, who had been seated on the floor by the stove all this time playing with a rag doll, paying no attention to the raised voices.

In the morning we started off again to walk to New Westminster, which I here learnt was the largest town on the mainland of British Columbia. We followed the line of railroad, walking along the track, and passing on numberless bridges across streams and sloughs through a flat timbered country. That day we made thirty-six miles, camping at last in a fencemakers' camp, where two white men were superintending a large gang of Chinamen engaged in fencing off the line. It was bitterly cold and very late when we got to the camp, but the two white men gave us some coffee and sat talking with us for some time, though their conversation's tendency was not encouraging, as they ran down New Westminster, averring that it was unlikely any one would get work in such a dead-looking town. Finally, they went to their little tent, while I raked up some more wood for the fire and lay down beside it, to wake at intervals all night long shivering with the cold. My partner made a little shelter of a pile of ties near at hand, and shivered there by himself till early dawn, when he came out to me, seating himself over the fire like an Indian, with the water running out of his rather weak eyes, making clean channels down his unwashed face, for he did not, I imagine, very often wash.

This day another long walk over flats, and we came out to the river Fraser, now broad and placid, with islands and bars in it piled with drift-wood and brush, and long back washes half as broad as the river, but shallow and weedy. Then to Harrison River, bright and clear and blue, a Fraser tributary, and dinner at a Chinaman's restaurant, where we had a plentiful and well-cooked meal served by the owner himself, who spoke good English to us, Chinese to his pig-tailed compatriots, and fluent Chinook to his Indian wife, who held in her arms a curious child with the characteristics of Indian and Chinaman stamped unmistakably upon it. The father admired it immensely, and was, it seemed, very fond of his wife who, for her part, was stolid and undemonstrative, as most pure-bred Indians are, except when under the influence of liquor.

Then away again over the long bridge, and that night we stayed with an oldish French farmer, who lived on a swamp in a new wooden house all by himself, and he served us well, and talked queer French to me and strange English, and made me very comfortable, charging next to nothing for it, making our thanks for our night's entertainment hearty and not merely perfunctory. And at noon we were at the Mission, eighteen miles from New Westminster, and there we determined to wait for the steamer, having had enough walking. So we stayed at a boarding-house for our meals, and slept in an old disused mill, where the wind had free entrance through cracks and joints and warped seams, and the ceilings and ties and joints were covered with long cobwebs, and an infrequent rat came out squeaking for the flour and grain that were wont to be but were there no more. And I slept, eking out my thin blankets with dirty old sacks. Next afternoon the 'Gem' steamer came down stream. Poor little wretched steamer to be so miscalled: 'Coalscuttle' or 'Hog-pen' would have made good names for her. The captain and one more made up the crew—two all told. The captain usually steered, and the other man engineered and fired up, and one or the other would rush out when making a landing to hitch a rope round a stump; and when wood ran low they would run her ashore near a pile, the noble skipper getting out to throw half a cord on deck. Then they had to take it aft before they could back her off. So we made slow progress, even with the current of the noble river under us, especially as every little while we stopped to take a few squealing pigs on board or some sacks of potatoes.

We had a few fellow-passengers, one of whom, a Mr. Turnbull, kept a temperance hotel in New Westminster. I had a talk with him, and finding that he was, to all appearance, a really good-hearted man, I determined to stay at his place and bestow my last dollar or two on him, for my cash was now nearly run out.

The scenery on the river was placid but beautiful. The hills were not high as a general rule, but still two or three ranges were in sight that were mountains. And far above all in the distance glittered the silver, snowy, truncated, volcanic cone of Mount Baker, solitary and alone, in Washington Territory, for we were now near the southern border of British Columbia. This peak rose above the clouds, towering 10,000 feet and even more. And there were long bright reaches of waters before us, with willows trailing on the banks, and every now and again we saw a stretch of back water, silent and still, windless, with reflections in its depths, while before and around us the dancing waters of our flowing river threw back the sunlight. And we were now in tidal waters On the right the frowning Pitt River Mountains and the entrance to the Pitt River. In front we saw a white building—a cannery for salmon—and round the bend the town, built on the river front, and running up towards the crest of a hill that showed a gaunt fringe of pines and firs, robbed of their foliage and branches by a forest fire. And beneath them fields of stumps and clearings.

And we came to the solitary dark wharves, which made one imagine that this had been once a busy town, and was now living in the memory of the past and the hope of the future, like a bear in its winter cavern, supported by its accumulations of summer fatness, and dreaming of the berries of the later springtime.

And so to the Farmers' Home. Saturday night, and November 2. I was but sixteen miles from the sea, the Gulf of Georgia. In a little over seven months I had come from New York, having journeyed nearly 8,000 miles in train, on steamer, and on foot; over prairie, mountain, river, and lake; in pain, and misery, in joy and delight, with Fear and Hope my companions; and now I could in imagination hear the roar of the breakers of the ancient ocean of the Pacific and smell the sweet brine odour of its illimitable waters that rolled to Australia and Japan, and between these, as through wide-opened gates, against the dark African continent half a world away.

I left the wharves and passed up dark Front Street to Main Street, bustling and well lighted, and I was in the Farmers' Home, looking a strange wild man of the woods amongst the well-dressed citizens of the place, who sat round the fire in the smoking-room, discussing with eagerness a murder at the jail, for that day one jailer had shot another. And my first comment would have been a strange one to a civilised ear. I thought, 'What a fuss about a murder! This is evidently not Texas, and killings are scarce.' And so it is in British Columbia; murders are comparatively rare, and Judge Begbie is a hanging judge, who is feared by the wilder emigrants and settlers and citizens, whites, English or Canadian or American, the Indians and the Chinese. I sat down among them in silence, but soon found a congenial spirit in a man who had travelled, who spoke up when I ventured to express my surprise at there being so much excitement about a solitary murder, and we soon found that we were agreed on the point. In the course of a violent discussion that followed we mischievously supported the Texas and Southern method of relying on pistol arbitration. 'At any rate,' said Johnson, my new friend, 'if a man gets into a row in Texas he won't be kicked and jumped on, and it is better to be shot. And a man there does not rely on his superior brute strength, for a small man is just as likely to be smart with weapons as a giant, or smarter.' Then, as talk began to be rather hot, I turned the conversation to work, and found out that there was small chance of getting any if it were not on the railroad work at Port Moody or Port Hammond, unless I should happen to be lucky enough to fall into a job at one of the three saw-mills in the town. And then my inquiries elicited that there was a library in the town. My dreams were true then! And there were actually chess-players to be found there! So when I got tired out I went to bed and dreamed I was in the library at the British Museum, and that afterwards I played chess with Zukertort at Simpson's in the Strand and beat him badly.

CHAPTER XIV.

NEW WESTMINSTER.

SUNDAY I spent in letter-writing, in conversation, or sulky sullenness—or, better and more euphemistically —contemplation, retrospect, and forecasting. Prophesying unto myself from the past gave little hope of good, so my last mental resource was proverbs, such as 'It's a long lane that has no turning' and 'Every cloud has a silver lining,' and so on. Here I was down again to one and a half dollars, in a strange place, with no friends save my no-account partner from up country, who had no more money than I. It began to seem to me that I was a very wanderer, a male Io driven by gadflies from plain to mount and mount to sea and strait; that I was a footless bird, not of Paradise but of an Inferno; that I was a thistledown on an endless wind, with never a friendly eddy to drop me down to root and grow, though it were but to a thistle. And I bethought myself that I had consumed eight months in travelling, that I had seen much and suffered much, and rejoiced much as well, and that it was at last time for me to stay for awhile and gather in shekels, if it were in any way possible, else it would be perennial seed-sowing by the wayside and never a harvest, and no harvest-home with songs of sweet thanksgiving and return. So I said, 'If I can but turn my hand to something in this town, however humble and ill-paid it be, here I will stay; for my health is better, and it is time I fed my mind with something over and beyond scenery of pines and peaks, of cloud and mist and dew, and the wonderful music of the organic winds of the worlds and the Psalm of Nature to the unknown God.'

Therefore, next day, when my cash amounted to twenty-five cents, I sought and found work in a saw-mill—hard and laborious lifting of timbers, arranging of boards and planks, carting and carrying of saw-dust, flooring boards, beadings and scrollings, sashes, doors, what not. Twelve hours a day, minus one half hour for a hurried dinner—6 A.M. to 6 P.M.; enough for a giant, enough for me, and at first more than enough. Board and thirty dollars a month for this labour, every cent earned, and more than earned surely, by sweat and fatigue of muscle, and contact with Chinamen—that strange, indomitable, persevering, vile, and wonderful race.

So to work I went, and was very nearly discharged the first morning by the superintendent, who declared that he knew not what had come over men who came to the coast from the east, for they all wanted a 'soft seat,' a 'soft snap,' which is, being interpreted, a light and easy job. Wrongly enough in my case, however, as he found out when he sent me into the mill to work with a mighty man from Michigan—M'Culloch, one of the finest Americans I ever knew—strong, long and lithe, quick of motion, quick of eye, large-handed and large-limbed, clean-coloured, moustached and otherwise shaved, with the pupil of one eye pear-shaped, making him strange as a man with eyes of two colours, like the Hereward of Kingsley's, sharp and lively in speech, kindly of heart, liberal in opinion, atheist, human, and lovable.

Next a young sawyer, Johnny—little Johnny, as we called him—small and bright, and strong as a young bull when he got hands and knees under a log or 'cant' of lumber; a fighter, and a ready one; pugnacious as a gamecock, and quick as lightning with his small hands, but pleasant and friendly if one who cared not for quarrels watched the glint of his eyes and made an occasional soft answer to this wrathful bantam.

Then Indians, half-breeds and Chinamen mingled and ever changing, and the chief sawyer beyond, a deceitful man, a speaker behind backs. Between him and Johnny great enmity existed as it seemed.

In such company in the half-open mill, one storey up in air, I passed the days, with the whirr of belts above and below, the scream of the circular saws as they bit the advancing log of pine or spruce or

Douglas fir, with the strips of bitten-out wood thrown out in a stream, and clouds of smaller sawdust, with the smiting of mallets on wedges in the cut, and the heavy fall on the greasy skids of the divided tree. And then, in the pool below, stood a long figure with a pole balancing on a round log, pushing it into its place, then the hammer driving in iron clamps or dogs, and the chain, revolving on the drum, dragging the ponderous tree to the saw, and then its rolling over and over on to the carriage, and afterwards more saw-screaming and sawdust and wedge-driving. So hour after hour, till the trees, rude and huge, fall into planks and boards and squared timbers—large for bridges or small for posts or pickets, and the waste cut into laths, and the sawdust burning in the gaping furnaces to drive the saw again. Then sudden whistle screaming, and hurrying figures, while the saws revolve slower and slower, and all is still, so that one can hear his own voice, and the hum of the saw only lingers in the unaccustomed ear; then dinner devoured, not eaten, and a smoke, and the whistle, and the saws turn quicker and quicker, and all is to do again till dark and supper and rest.

So went the life, and the days were quick and laborious. The superintendent spoke to M'Culloch one day:

'What kind of a man is that long fellow with the big hat?'

'Well, Mr. G——, he does not know much about

saw-mills, but I just tell you he is a rustler. He gets round quicker'n any man in the mill, in spite of his long legs.'

'Why, I nearly fired him the first morning; I must have made a mistake. I thought he wasn't any good.'

Now a 'rustler' is a great Western word, and expresses much. It means a worker, an energetic one, and no slouch can be a rustler. So this was high praise. And ' fired ' means, in that oversea, overland language, being discharged, so Mr. G—— did not mean me any good. But when he saw I could work we were friends, and he did me many a good turn.

We slept, some four or five of us, over the dining-room, and the rest lived in cabins, or little huts, some of them boarding themselves, being married either to white women or Indians, or perhaps not married. My friend in our sleeping-room was a German—Pete— a great character, who had lived many years in California, and who had been working at various intervals at the mill and up country at other saw-mills, or at pile-driving or bridge-making, just to make, so he said, 20 dols. and a suit of clothes to go back to California with. But when the 20 dols. were collected he would disappear and be found sitting in front of a hotel, blandly inviting passers-by to take a drink, and when the money was dissipated he would come back to make it over again, being in deep dumps and very virtuous for the future. He had been seven years trying to make the money and the clothes, but though he was always dressed well enough he could not get that new suit and the dollars both at the same time. Pete was a great favourite of mine.

The library, of course, I did not leave long unattacked. The third day, after working-time, brought me to it, and there were actually lots of books and some boards and chessmen, and, better still, men playing. I went in, dressed as usual in my working garb, having no other, and sat down to watch a game which was being contested between a man with weak eyes, who had a great grievance, as I afterwards found out, and a man named Collins, with whom I got to be quite friendly. Both played fairly well, but I knew I could beat them. I had been a fourth-class player in London, and had played regularly at Gatti's in the old chess corner, in the Adelaide Gallery, for more than two years, so I was probably more than a match for any Western player. When the game was over, and the man with a grievance had aired it for half an hour, talking vehemently because he had been deprived of the librarianship of this very place, I asked his opponent if he would give me a game. He looked at me out of the corners of his eyes, as if wondering if I could play. And I took the vacant chair. First game was won in less than twenty minutes. My opponent looked at me, as if he thought I had made a great mistake. The next one was played by him more carefully, and it took me three-quarters of an hour to mate him. Then a look of stern resolution came over his face, and he put his head in his hands and studied every move. But I beat him in an hour. He sighed and looked dazed, but shook hands with me and said I was the best player in British Columbia.

Then, to console him, I told him how I had learnt to be a player, and that I had actually, by a fluke, twice beaten a man who had once, by a fluke, beaten Zukertort. He looked greatly relieved. I very often played with him afterwards, and let him win a game now and again to keep him in good temper.

Then I went through the bookshelves, with the librarian showing me a light, and I saw enough to make me promise to be a subscriber, at the moderate terms of 50 cents, or 2s. 1d., a month. I brought up the money next evening and took home Buckle's ' History of Civilisation,' a book I had never read through before. There were 2,000 volumes in the library, and during the time I stayed in New Westminster I devoured most of those that were worth reading, for there was a vast amount of engineering and military matter, left by the English troops who were formerly stationed in the locality, which had no interest for me.

Then on Sundays I would take a walk, sometimes with a companion, though usually alone, and sit down on the river bank and look at the stream and the scenery beyond it, or climb the hill at the back of the town, whence I could see Mount Baker's white cone across miles, yes, fifty miles of forest, high and shining or, turning towards the west, catch sight of the glitter of the straits, and beyond, the peaks of Vancouver against the blue. East, thirty miles away, stood the Pitt River mountains, snow covered, beautiful and near in the clear transparent air. But first glance with me at the river, on our right broad and clear and wider than the Thames at Westminster, and across it at these narrow flats, with a few shanties on them scattered here and there, with blue wreaths of smoke above their chimneys, and a long low white cannery, reflecting the sun, under the gentle slope of a hill covered with fir and pine. Then see how the river spreads out above this to twice its breadth below, bending away to the right until it takes no reflections, but throws out sparkles from the ripples of a solitary gust of wind and in a moment is lost to sight, while beyond its farther bank rises slope after slope of the hills beyond the Pitt River until, on the left, the high peaks are snow against the blue heavens, and the long shoulder of the dim range runs down in curve and sudden lower peak to hide the farther fainter hills of Sumass.

Ah, how beautiful it was, even for a discontented being like myself!

So, working and dreaming, time ran on till well into December, and winter came on us with rush of white wings and icy breath. First the hills covered themselves with snow, and the north-east wind came down the reaches of the river, blowing into the open mill like the wind of death, making me rush out for increase of clothes, until at last I worked in all the shirts I possessed and coat and waistcoat. Then cakes and floes of ice came down stream, and came back again with the flood tide; there was grinding of huge blocks against the shore and piling up of jamming floes in mid water; and perpetual roar for days till the bitterer frost suddenly spanned the stream with cold fingers, fixed it, and grew in power of solid dominion up and down, growing thick and strong. And snow came in the streets, drifting over and over; from the houses depended stalactites and icicles four feet long, and blunt stalagmites grew up below.

Upon the hilly streets in town, boys and girls were laughing, shouting and screaming, running down hill in sleighs, 'coasting' as they call it, with swift velocity, sometimes capsizing without much harm done. And we had time enough for play, for the logs were set fast in the thick ice and the 'buzz-saw' was silent, the fires out, and snow upon the piles of sawed lumber. So we ate and drank and slept, and I read through the library steadily: Gibbon's 'Rome' again, with story of Alaric and the grave of the Busentinus, and Attila the Hun and Mahomet and the Turk, in the slow majestic sentence; Vasari's 'Lives of the Painters,' graphic, inaccurate, delightful; and reading on without system, or attempt at any, Alison's 'History' and Motley's 'Netherlands,' terrible and picturesque, a favourite of my boyhood, and Buckle's book of destiny and necessity, 'The History of Civilisation.' Then a canter among the fields of science: Huxley on the 'Origin of Species,' and Darwin's book itself, the most delightful book of science, that puts all Nature into one's hand; and Carlyle's 'Essays,' and Landor, whose 'Æsop' and 'Rhodope' I learnt by heart almost, with its beautiful pathos and marvellous rhythm of unequalled prose. Then snatches of 'Noctes Ambrosianæ,' and Maginn's 'Miscellanies,' and Locke's 'Human Understanding' as a cold douche, and 'Middlemarch,' 'Bleak House,' and my favourite novel of novels, the 'Tale of Two Cities.' So I filled up my time, at any rate not to disadvantage, save that the bitter weather and my greed for books kept me indoors without exercise, and this was to be revenged on me afterwards. And then came to me, from England, Virgil and Horace, for which I had sent, and I dipped here and there in these.

So Christmas came and passed away, and it was the dead of winter.

During all this fearfully cold weather, of ice and snow and bitter wind, we lived in the room above the dining-room without any fire. G——, the superintendent, told us several times that we could get a stove and stove-pipe from the carpenter's shop if we liked to put it up ourselves. But no, we were absolutely too lazy to do it, and used to lie in bed nearly all day, or stand round the pipe that came through our floor from the room below when that stove was lighted.

We would walk about with blankets round us, looking like Indians, and sometimes we went in for making a noise—dancing, singing, and fooling, just to keep warm. And we actually went through it all without a stove until the thaw came, and then we got it and made big fires. 'Pete,' said I, 'we are deuced cunning fellows and show lots of foresight. It will be cold next winter.'

Our room, too, was often a sight to look at, especially when we had a row about whose turn it was to sweep out, with the result of general sulkiness and declarations that 'I won't' and 'I won't,' until somebody got desperate and hurled a mass of dust and rubbish, chips and rags, down the stairs. So we were tormented with fleas for our folly, and had uncomfortable days and nights through laziness.

On December 29 some one proposed a walk over to Granville, or Burrard's Inlet. I wish he had been hanged before he suggested it. But I thought a tramp would do me good, for I had been suffering from vile headaches for some days before. So I and Pete, and John Anderssen, a Swede, and Charley, my partner from the upper country, and another Swede set out after breakfast in the snow. It was hard walking, going crunch, crunch in it; but still the road had been beaten down a little, and one could find reasonably good footing if walking in Indian file.

About eleven o'clock we came to Granville, and walked down to the mill and long wharves, where ships loaded lumber for South America and Australia. Then the wind began to blow, and it was fearfully chill and bitter, searching me through and through as it swept over the Inlet, a kind of fiord, laden with concentrated frost. Some of us ate dinner, though I had little appetite, for my head was nearly splitting, and I rejected all tobacco, sure sign of something very wrong in a man who had used it for ten years. Then we set out homeward at two o'clock. And what a walk it was! At first we kept close together, talking; then we plodded along in silence, as the low sun at last disappeared with pale glow of gold, and the gibbous moon stood out half way up the sky before us, brighter, it seemed, than the sun. Yet we had not done half our homeward twelve miles. We began to get thirsty, terribly thirsty, and some took up snow and chewed it; but I thought it was not good, as I fancied I had read so in some book of travels, and still plodded on with my tongue nearly as dry as it had been on some horrible days of travel in sunburnt New South Wales. And it grew colder and colder still in this forest. The wind had dropped and it was calm and still, but the frost grew out on the bushes into diamonds, glittering before us on twig and pendulous snowy branch, and the unbroken snow on both sides shone with innumerable millions of sharp spicules, keen and crystalline. The moon cast blackened shadows on the white, and her splendour came down on us with such lack of warmth that her light seemed a ghostly cataract of freezing water, and the sharp stars stabbed us with spears of cold when we came out of the shadow of the forest.

Then came a faint shout from behind. Tired as I was, I turned back. Pete was seated on a log, swearing he was going to die; Anderssen lay in the middle of the road in snow and moonlight, chewing snow with his head down, talking unintelligible Swedish and mixed English, and cursing. I sat down by the ditch at the side of the road and put some snow to my burning forehead. We must have seemed a queer crowd in that silent forest.

Presently Pete. 'Charley, I can't get up, I'm stuck fast to this log. Am I going to stay here and be frozen to a snow image?' 'You can if you like,' I said, sulkily and selfishly; 'I'm not, if I can rustle through it.' I got up, fell on my knees, and rolled into the snow at the bottom of the ditch. 'Come and pull me out, Pete.' 'Can't get up,' said Pete solemnly. 'You then, John,' to Anderssen. John growled and lay still. 'You hog,' said I, 'quit chewing that snow; you'll die there if you don't.' John muttered: 'I die in the road and you in the ditch.' Then the other Swede came across and held his hand to me, and I scrambled out of the brush and snow. I went over to Anderssen and kicked him gently in the ribs: 'Get up, or I'll knock seven bells out of you. Give me your hand.' I got him up, and we pulled Pete off his log. 'Now,' I said, 'you may lie down and die; I won't come back any more. Good-bye.' So I and the other Swede set off again, plodding desperately, for I really felt as if I must have a drink or die myself, and I would not touch the snow. Presently we came through a patch of dead timber, and saw the lights of the town two miles away at the bottom of the slope. Half a mile farther brought us to a little log-house, where two woodcutters lived. In we went, and I drank about a quart of icy water, and out again. I was tired now, and my head was nearly bursting, with my temples throbbing hard. Every step I took seemed as if it was my last, for I thought I was shod with lead, and my legs were heavy and half dead. And the cold grew worse and worse. At last we came down to the flat, and another quarter of a mile brought me to our boarding-house. I stayed and turned off, my partner the Swede said nothing, marching straight ahead up town. I got to the door of the dining-room, turned the handle, and fell inside on my hands and knees, very much surprising two of the bosses, one of whom was Mr. G——. He said: 'Hullo, got back, eh?' I couldn't answer him at first, but I got up, shut the door, and fell on a bench near at hand. He saw I was about done, and he very kindly got me a cup of tea from the kitchen. Then he asked where Pete and the others were. 'Coming along behind if they're not dead yet,' I said, and then I went upstairs, threw my boots off with a great effort, fell into my bed, and drew the blankets over me. In five minutes the blood was running through all my veins like molten lead, and I was in a high fever. I fell asleep and did not wake till morning. Looking up I saw Pete in bed. 'You're not dead then, Pete?' said I, and he solemnly shook his head. 'Pretty near a go, though.'

I never felt cold like it in all my life, although it was not really very intense, as the thermometer in town did not go quite down to ten degrees below zero, which is nothing to the temperature at Kamloops and farther east, where it sometimes goes down to 30° and 40° below, or at Winnipeg in Manitoba, where 60° below is not uncommon in winter. I suppose I suffered more than I should otherwise have done, owing to my being in a very bad state of health at that time. For two weeks after this I was ill, for five days in bed, living on biscuits and milk. Then I recovered somewhat for another week or two, and then went down completely with bilious fever, and lay nearly dead for three weeks, coming round at last, when I was but a long ghost and a skeleton.

During this winter, when I was reasonably well, both before and after the fever, I used sometimes to go down to see some of the men who lived in the little cabins close at hand. This was an Indian town as well, and the Indians and whites used to live together in a fearful state of dirt and drunkenness. Indian women have few of them any notion of modesty left now, since the whites came amongst them, and the consequent license resulting from the state of manners was curious to see. Sometimes I walked into a cabin to find everybody drunk, perhaps some on the bed, some on the floor, or under the table ; or there would be a wild hubbub inside, with fragments of English, Chinook, German or Spanish, or the real guttural Indian with its strange clicks. On coming in, drink would be offered me, or I would be invited to send for some, and the 'jamberee' would get worse and worse, until finally there was a fight or a scratching match and loud oaths and yells.

One of the mill-men, an English sailor, went about continually with a black eye or his face scratched with the 'ten commandments,' until at last he was relegated to the discipline and sobriety of the jail for a period of three months for having broken open the door of an Indian woman to assault her on account of some fanciful amatory grievance. Sometimes the constable would make a raid and take a woman to jail for being drunk, but this was in the daytime, for he dared not come down round where we lived in the dark, as several had sworn vengeance on him if ever they caught him there when they had a chance of getting away without being discovered.

Thus my time passed away with sickness, riot, disorder, reading, and writing. Yes, writing too, for I wrote this winter an autobiography, psychological at that, with snatches of verse and long letters to England. This MS. I sent to a literary friend of mine in London, but it never came into his hand, having been lost in the post. Then I learnt some Chinook, so that I could speak a little to the Indians. And a strange enough jargon it is—English, French, and Indian; and English and French corrupted and altered to suit the vocal Indian peculiarities, or becoming l, as 'dly' for 'dry.' There are some strange words, as 'hyas puss-puss' for the mountain lion or cougar, the northern representative of the South American puma; 'hyas' means great or large; and 'hyin,' plenty. 'Moos-moos' is cow, and 'moos-moos glease,' butter. The great salutation is, 'Clahya, tilicum,' or 'How goes it, partner?' 'Siwash' is an Indian, and 'sitcum siwash' a half-breed. I never progressed very far in this gibberish, but I could say 'yes' and 'no,' 'nawitka' and 'halo,' and, 'What do you want?' 'Ikta mika tiki?' and so on, and gestures and English did the rest.

And then the frost broke up, and soon the mill was running again, and the river swung to and fro with burden of ice blocks, grinding on shingle and against wharf and pile. But I was yet weak and did little work for a fortnight, spending my time leisurely and in repose or in the library, until I got fat again and turned to throwing board and plank—fir, pine, cedar, and spruce—like a machine as before. And I was now in debt to the mill, and had to work a month to get out of the obligation ; and, besides, I owed a doctor's bill. So I had not, so far, made much more money by staying in one place. It was now February, I had been nearly four months in New Westminster, and was 30 dols. worse off than nothing. However, I felt reasonably contented, having some little leisure, for we did not run full time, and besides, something was always going wrong with the machinery or the belts, which gave me opportunities to get to chess or books.

But I doubt if I should have been in such a serene state of mind if the mill had owed me money, for it seemed they were in a bad way financially. If a man left it was hard, nay, almost impossible, to get what was due to him; and even when they discharged any one it was necessary for him to wait days to get a few miserable dollars. One man worried the manager so for his money, which was only 40 dollars, that at last H—— threatened to kick him off the place if he troubled him any more! Then another man wanted his, and H—— offered him an order for it on the Victoria agency of the firm. 'But how am I to get to Victoria without a cent?' said the unfortunate individual. 'Oh, get on board the "Teaser" and beat your way,' or, more literally and in English, cheat the steamer by stowing away. Strange advice under the circumstances truly! The Chinamen employed in the mill struck work until they got their money, which was found for them with great difficulty. Some of the creditors, men in the town, merchants and others, could only get payment by taking lumber for it, and the mill was constantly being sued in the courts, and we looked every day for somebody to come down and take the mill in execution, or something equally desperate. In fact, someone seized 120,000 feet on a schooner loading for Victoria. So I thought it lucky they did not owe me anything.

By the middle of March I began to make a little, and it grew up slowly to about 20 dols., which, considering the little likelihood there was of my getting it, seemed a huge sum. However, I determined to make it 30 dols., and then try to get paid in cash, not in clothes and hats out of the stores. But an incident happened that prevented the sum to my credit going beyond 23 dols., and that was in all probability the best thing for me under the circumstances, as if I had let it go to 30 dols. I should never have got any of it. It was the first week in April, and we were all at dinner, twenty at the table at which I sat and about ten at the other, with a Chinaman to wait on us and two cooking. Now this waiter was a very insolent individual, rather strong, with well-developed arms, who had for some time worked in the mill. He was the cause of my leaving the place. Wanting some more meat, I asked him for some civilly enough, I am sure, but none came. Thinking he might have forgotten, I asked again, and still no meat in any reasonable time. The final result was that I thrashed the man, and some one ran to the office and told H——, the manager, that I was killing a Chinaman. Just as I sat down in he rushed. 'Who's been making this disturbance?' 'I have,' I said. 'Then I discharge you.' 'That's all right about discharging, Mr. H——,' said I, 'but can I get my money?' 'You can get it this afternoon,' and out he went.

'Served the Chinaman right, old man,' said Mac and Johnny, 'but we're sorry you've got to go.' Then they and another went to the office, and wanted to know if the Chinaman was to be discharged too. 'No,' said H——. 'Well,' said Mac, the spokesman, 'if he isn't discharged we'll all go and shut the mill down.' So the Chinaman went too, and Fraser, the book-keeper, who was a very good friend of mine, actually charged him with two cups, a plate, and a tin dipper which had been smashed when we were in the thick of the fight, and, what's more, made him pay for them.

And thus it was I left the mill, for I did get my money, though the manager had to borrow 20 dols. to pay me. It was lucky that it happened as it did, for in about ten days the concern went bankrupt, and nobody got any money at all.

That night I went up town, taking good care to look about me as I went through the Chinese quarter, and bade farewell to my chess and library acquaintances, and in the morning, after long deliberation as to whether I should take the 'Teaser' to Victoria or the 'Adelaide' for Yale, I made up my mind to the latter course, and started for Kamloops again to visit my old boss, from whom I had received many kindly letters since arriving in the town of New Westminster.

CHAPTER XV.

BACK TRACKS TO EAGLE PASS.

So I was bound up-stream once more, leaving saw-mill and library behind me. Yet I carried a few books, for I had Virgil and Horace, and a volume or two of poetry, Coleridge and Keats, and 'Academy Skits' for '84, and the illustrated catalogue of the Institute of Water-Colour Painters, which had been sent to me, and which I was now taking up to give to Hughes. So my blankets were heavier than when I came down, for I had even left my 'Sartor Resartus' with him as a present, as I thought I might do myself good by a change, especially as I nearly knew it by heart, having read it through many thousand miles of travel; to say nothing of my habit of poring over that same volume at breakfast when in England, to which, without meaning any disrespect to Carlyle, I believe I owed more than a moiety of my indigestion and congestion of liver.

And I was in the Fraser again, this time to fight the current for a hundred miles or so to Yale. And it was a very pleasant trip. Our captain, one of the well-known pioneer families of British Columbia, a Moore, the one-armed one, was a very delightful companion, and Jim, the mate, was as good. Then we had two Chilliwhack farmers, and one from Sumass, and a Chinaman or two. When we tied up for the night at the bank below Chilliwhack, for we started late, we sat down and talked and smoked most amicably, and when they found out I could sing, it was 'Sing us another,' 'Come and take a drink, you must be dry,' and then sing again; and then Jim and the skipper beguiled the intervals by telling dreadful stories of going up the Fraser and getting steam up to 150 lb., when the boiler was only certified for 60 lb. Then he told a yarn about the steamer that blew up under similar conditions ten miles or so below Yale, and another of the boat we were then in, when they one day had the tiller-ropes break in the most perilous place on the river, and had to let her drift blindly, till she hung in an eddy behind a rock, giving them a chance to mend the gear. Then we sang more songs and had more drinks till twelve o'clock, and I spread my blankets out and went to sleep, with the consciousness that I had done my duty in singing at any rate, for I was as hoarse as I could be.

In the morning there was a frightful fog of mist and smoke, caused mostly, however, by the latter, which came from a glorious mountain fire above Pitt River, which we had seen the night before.

The whole side of the mountain was red hot, and the horseshoe ring of the outer flames shone gloriously bright, while there was a mile of dull ember in the midst of it.

In consequence of this fog we had to go very slowly, at times stopping altogether, and at last, when we thought, or rather the captain thought, for I had no notion at all, that we were near Chilliwhack, the deck-hands shouted, and someone answered out of the fog, and next moment we went bump against the high bank, stem foremost, and soon made a landing, and parted with two of our friends.

Then it gradually cleared up, and we ran on, fighting the stream at intervals, but 'making the riffle,' or crossing the rapid, without resorting to bacon hams in the furnace or a nigger on the safety-valve, as was the custom in the palmy days of steamboat racing on the Mississippi or the Sacramento. And then we ran through lovely reaches of calm water, and past huge piles of drift-wood stuck on sand-bars, and came to Hope, whence the trail runs to Similkameen, the last new gold find in British Columbia. After that came fierce fighting with the stream, and again we tied up and waited for morning; then riffle after riffle was triumphantly passed, the whistle-scream echoed from the entrance of the cañon, and I was at Yale once more, somewhat exercised in mind as to the means of getting to Kamloops without walking and without paying my fare, which was too much for my pocket. Now the main office of the railroad was then at Yale, where A. Onderdonk, the well-known and much-abused contractor, whom the men usually called Andy or A. O., had his residence, and it was often possible to get a pass up country to work on the road, either grading or track-laying, without paying for it. I had no intention of working at this kind of work if it were possible to do without it, for I now considered myself a cut above a mere railroader, being a saw-mill man, for railroading is considered by all who do not follow it as a 'low-down job,' nearly as bad as the dog's-meat man's in London. So I went up to the office and bored two or three officials, even speaking to the great Andy himself, who is a good-looking and pleasant individual, until at last I was told to jump on the train in the morning for Ashcroft or Barnes, near the Black Cañon, where I could get work.

Down I went early, with my blankets on my back, having slept that night at Taylor's, where the usual racket and fandango had been going on, and found a dozen or two others who were bound for the same place on the same terms, and besides these I came across Fraser from the mill, who was going up to Eagle Pass to be book-keeper for a contractor doing grading and tunnelling along the banks of the Big Shushwap Lake. We got in the train and started up the cañon. I was glad enough to get to Ashcroft, or at any rate out of the worst of the cañon, for the narrow shelf of rock on which we ran, the vast blocks of overhanging stone, the perilous high-trestle bridges, and the black depth of howling waters beneath, kept me in a state of mental tension, especially when we slashed round a curve or went down an occasional sharp descent that made me imagine the train was flying in the air. We got out at Ashcroft, in the Alkali Dry Belt, but I put my blankets on my back and marched a mile to Barnes's Hotel, and slept there that night, after having had the worst supper I ever paid 50 cents for, spending the evening in a crowded bar-room amid noise and smoke and half-intoxicated railroad men from the camps near at hand. In the morning I started on my walk to Hughes's Ranche, which was about forty-one miles from here. I passed my companions of yesterday working with pick and shovel in a mixed gang of whites and Chinamen, and tramped along the railroad track between the rails, for the line was now roughly finished as far as Savona's Ferry, at the foot of Kamloops Lake. It was a weary, thirsty walk, for it was almost impossible to step except upon the ties or sleepers, and these were set so that to go from one to the next made me walk with a ridiculous short step, and if I missed out one I made an immense stride. And I could not step in between, for the line was unballasted; that is, the space between the ties was not filled up with earth or gravel. Then there was no path alongside the track; or if there was, it was painful to walk upon on account of the rocks. The water in the little creeks that ran down the hollows in the hills was terribly alkaline, soft and horrible to taste, so that as I tramped on the awkward ties, watching every step, with a burning sun glaring on the bare soil, I grew thirstier and thirstier, while the beautiful blue stream of the Thompson, down far below me, or shining farther off yet in the distance, mocked my parching tongue, and the musical whisper of the water, as it ran over the rapids, sounded like a fiend's rejoicing voice. So I stumbled along, tasting almost every stream I came to, unless I saw the white alkaline incrustation on its banks, in the hope of finding good water. But in the twenty-one or twenty-two miles to Savona I only found one that was passable. I tramped into that little settlement, or rather into the newer portion, since called Van Horn, after one of the C.P.R. officials, at three o'clock, 'peted,' done up. I came to a Chinaman's, who had 'Restaurant' painted outside, with some Chinese characters as well, and walked in. I began to demand dinner in the usual way one speaks to Chinamen there, but found he could talk very good English indeed. He gave me a good dinner too, and I sat there smoking and talking till half-past four, and then started, hoping to get to Hughes's that night, although the distance was seventeen miles. If I had taken the wagon-road I might have done it, but thinking it would be shorter to follow the railroad along the lake until I came to Cherry Creek, which ran down through his land, I kept on the track, taking the bare grade, until that gave out at places and I had to scramble round bluffs or rocks, until it was dark, and I came to a camp where there was only one man, who refused me a cup of tea. I thanked him for his courtesy, and started to climb the hill in the dark to discover the wagon-road, as it would have been out of my way to go farther on the grade. At last I found the road, and set out on the last six miles in total darkness, but when I had done three, arriving at Roper's, I felt I was done up and could do no more. So I opened the door of the hotel and walked into the bar-room. Next morning I left for Hughes's and took three hours to do three miles, such was my fatigue from the day before. I found Hughes working by the house, shook hands with him, and went and lay down, enjoying *dolce far niente* for that day at any rate. I stayed there some days, working a little, sometimes shooting, and sometimes trout-fishing, for there was a plentiful supply of small brook-trout to be caught there, and one afternoon I hooked out forty.

Then I went into Kamloops and stayed a day or two to look out for work, but seeing no chance I came back for a little while and then went again. Finally, acting on my friend's advice, I determined to go up to Eagle Pass again, as work was reported lively there, and a town building up rapidly. My 23 dols. was now nearly exhausted, and when I got into town I had insufficient to pay my fare up to the lakes, and so I went to the captain of the 'Kamloops' steamer, and he allowed me to work my passage up. So down I went to the fires, and passed wood for the fireman, stowing it away whenever they took more on board, working like a demon. One time I stowed away three cords of four-foot wood without resting. First my shirt came off, then my undershirt, then I slung the wood without even that, with the perspiration rolling off me in streams, getting into my eyes, and running down into my very boots. It was little scenery I saw at that time, as I was down in the stoke-hole nearly all the while. At last we came up to the landing, and I could hardly recognise the place. Instead of three buildings there were more than a hundred, all strung along the foreshore, and new ones were going up, and everywhere one could hear hammers going and the axe, while on the beach was a crowd of men, and piles of merchandise, of lumber, casks and odds and ends innumerable. Had it not been for the unchanged mountain background I could not have thought it was the almost desolate spot I came to after my tramp over the Selkirks and through the Golden Range.

I went ashore and up to Murdoch's, finding the place in the throes of dissolution and regeneration, pulling down and rebuilding at once. At every step I came across acquaintances from the lower country or men I had met in the Kicking Horse Pass. There seemed much business doing, especially for carpenters, who were in great request, and, judging from the number of drunken men, a vast quantity of liquor was being disposed of, although it was forbidden to sell it without a licence from the Provincial Government and with or without one by the Dominion Government, which led to a conflict, to which I shall refer afterwards. At the present time Murdoch was the only man with a licence, but still it was possible to buy whisky anywhere. I went into the bar-room, threw my blankets in a corner, shook hands with Murdoch and one or two acquaintances, sat down, lighted my perpetual clay pipe, and took in the scene and conversation. There was an immense amount of railroad talk, and I soon saw it would be easy enough to get work of that kind if other things failed. I determined not to do any of it if it could be avoided, and thinking that Fraser might be able to get me something to do, I went down to the end of the town and got an Irishman, voluble and semi-intoxicated, to pull me across the lake for four bits to where he was working. When I got across I found he was somewhere else, and waited for three hours, meanwhile getting most vilely hungry, and ageing as it were, for I soon suspected myself a fool, which would, according to the 'Night Thoughts,' indicate my age as thirty, and soon afterwards I seemed to know it, and that means forty. At last I could stand no longer to watch the salmon and lake trout leap for flies, and I got into another boat, paying another four bits to get back. So my trip was in vain, and cost me a dollar, which I could ill afford. On arriving at the landing I had a good supper and was rejuvenated, though I had now but half a dollar left, and half a dollar in the mountains of British Columbia only means one meal, or two drinks or four cigars, whereas in Melbourne it would have the larger significance of four dinners and a single extra glass of beer, and even in London Bohemia the initiated is a long way from starvation and the archways with 2s. 2d. to his credit, or even with but a splendid shilling.

So I was very pleased to meet Fraser in the main and only street that night, for I borrowed five dollars from him, which was given kindly and gracefully. Indeed, one thinks of five dollars there as one would think of five shillings at home, and I spent a dollar when I had plenty of them, which truly was only occasionally, as if mere silver was nothing. Fraser promised to see if it were possible to get me a good job with his contractor Mitchell; but next day I was fortunately put beyond any need of troubling him for work or further loans by getting employment at 2.50 dollars, or 10s. 5d. a day. My 'boss' was one of the best men to work for I ever met, a Mr. G. F. Kyle, a Canadian, who had risen to a good position in Onderdonk's employ. I never saw any one who had anything to say against him, but, on the contrary, everybody had a good word

P

for him. He was a tall, strong, pleasant and good-featured man, somewhat English looking, with a sharp eagle eye and that undefinable look about him of a man who knows other men—somewhat similar to the appearance and quick, penetrating glance of 'our only General,' whom I had often seen in Pall Mall and the War Office when he was Quartermaster-General. He made me work hard while there was any necessity for it, but then he worked himself, and was as energetic a 'rustler' as British Columbia held. My first month with him was one of almost continuous labour, Sunday and week-day and overtime, so that I made about eighty dollars that month, subject to the deduction of a dollar a day for board. We built a stable and a warehouse for the stores for the railroad work in the Eagle Pass, for the first twenty miles of which Kyle was superintendent. Then I grubbed up stumps, cleared up all round, graded off the yard into a slope, cut poles in the forest, helped load up the wagons, weighed the stores out—potatoes, bacon, and flour—marked them, and so on. So for that first month I had my hands full indeed. Beside Kyle there was a book-keeper, a Mr. Requa, who was also a very agreeable individual, and with whom I got along very well, so well indeed that he told me I was a first-rate worker and hadn't a lazy hair in my head. I said, 'Wait awhile, you don't know me yet, for I can be as lazy as the next man.' Then there was the storekeeper, little Mac, who had been a telegraph operator in the lower country. He was extremely conceited, and would tell me, 'I am so different from other fellows, you know, Charlie,' as indeed he was, but not in any way to give him much reason for boasting. Besides these there was an old white-haired watchman, with whom I had some trouble about the horses. He was going to break my neck, but it is still whole. There were also two teamsters, one a good-looking, somewhat soft young fellow, genial and pleasant, Bob by name or nickname, and Joe Fagin, tall, clumsy, with huge strength, being capable of lifting 800 lb., hairless on the face, ruddy and reasonably good-tempered, a great swimmer and a splendid driver. Then there were two carpenters, one of whom insisted I was a runaway man-o'-war's man. The other was a gambler, and dropped his money at stud-horse poker or faro as soon as he made it. These two went away as soon as the store was finished.

All this time building was going on rapidly in the town, and money was very plentiful and circulated freely. Half the town would be drunk at night, and there was a fight or two every evening, and black eyes were plentiful as dollars. The Swedes were the worst for drinking, getting intoxicated early in the morning. One day I came across six lying in a pile, close to our warehouse, by the edge of the lake. One was lying with his head down hill and his hair touching the water. I tried to put him right, but as he was a heavy man, weighing perhaps 14 stone, with another heavy fellow lying across him, I was unable to get him up. While pulling away at him I woke one of the others, who was the least drunk. 'Get up,' said I, 'and help me get your partner out; his head's nearly in the water.' 'So much the worse for him,' said the other sleepily, and dropped off to rest again. I put a hat over the man's face to keep the burning sun from him, but when I came round again he had taken it off. So I let him lie.

Then there was a well-known individual in town, a Welshman whom we all called Taffy, who rejoiced in perennial drunkenness and black eyes. He was always fighting and always getting whipped, but, as he kept on, I suppose he liked it. One day he called a carpenter, whom I knew, an opprobrious name, and got badly choked and beaten. Our method of fighting there was different from what is considered fair in England. When a man falls or is knocked down, his opponent gets on him, choking or thumping him with his fists, and sometimes, if any sticks or stones, 'clubs' or 'rocks,' are lying within reach, they are brought into action, and, besides, biting and eye-gouging are not considered absolutely wrong, though seldom resorted to. Consequently, as Taffy was usually too drunk to stand up, he got the worst of his perpetual combats, unless he came across an opponent who was drunker than himself. This, however, would be very rare, as any increased intoxication would result in sleep and quietness. When

Taffy got to that stage he went down to his boat and lay under a tarpaulin, and one day, when Mac, the storekeeper, and I found him there, we cut him adrift and sent him out into the lake, where he floated round for an hour or two, an object of universal interest.

While working here I used to see Major Rogers, the surveyor who had surveyed the line through the Kicking Horse Pass and the Selkirks. He had been in the mountains seven years at this task, and he and his men toiled and suffered fearfully at times. His two nephews were with him, and were fine, good-looking young fellows.

After my first month times were much easier for me, as I had very little to do except to attend to a few horses in the stable and help load the wagons; consequently I used to lie on a pile of grain sacks in the stores and read novels. Then we would go in swimming, perhaps twice a day, and I would take a walk up town, looking into the gambling saloons or chatting with my acquaintances, who were not a few. And then I got my old chum Scott again, from the Kicking Horse Pass, who had followed my footsteps over the Selkirks in company with Davidson. When I saw him he was purser on a lake steamer, the 'Lady Dufferin,' and we had a great palaver together. He told me that he and Davidson had often talked about 'Texas,' as he still called me, wondering what had become of me. He was glad to see me again, as glad as I was to see him. He had had a hard time crossing the trail, though not so bad as I, for his boots fortunately did not chafe him, and, besides that, his time on the trail had been shorter, owing to the extension of the wagon road. We met constantly after this, until at last he left the steamer, being unable to stand Bill Fortune any longer. This man, an uneducated Yorkshireman who was 'bossed' by his wife, was owner of a little saw-mill below Kamloops. He used to cause some amusement by blowing his little steamer's whistle at intervals from the time he came in sight round the point to the time he disappeared again, unless he was too much intoxicated to pull the rope. When Scott left his employ he took to running whisky into the town, but without much success, as the police confiscated his biggest venture, which almost ruined my friend, as he had put all his cash into it that time. I used to tell him it served him right for trying to make money out of whisky, for I was then, and am now, a prohibitionist, although not a total abstainer. I am quite sure that I went through sufferings and privations both in British Columbia and afterwards that would have almost killed a man accustomed to drink spirits, and I have often been six months at a time without drinking anything intoxicating, even when it almost risked my life to refuse. Nevertheless, in some company I have had to drink, and I myself have deemed it occasionally politic to swagger into a bar-room and say: 'Step up, boys, what's your liquor?' just to show a rough crowd I was not too 'high-toned' to drink with them, or too mean to pay out a dollar now and again.

It was getting towards the end of June, when one evening Kyle sent for me to say that he wanted me to come out with him the next day to bridge over some sloughs, and that he needed another man, too, who was to be an axeman. So I went round and hired one, and next morning this man, Williams, whom I had met before at Kamloops, and who was Taffy's partner, and I set out together up the road and were presently joined by Kyle on horseback. We all worked together, felling trees across these sloughs to make temporary bridges for the men to cross who were making the grade. We took all the morning to do three, and then Williams and the boss and I ate our lunch on one of the trees in the middle of the swamp, dipping up water in a tin cup to drink. I was not much of an axeman; indeed it is rare to find an Englishman who can do very much with that instrument, as it requires a long apprenticeship, so Kyle did great part of my work in showing me how to do it. He knew very well I worked hard, but then he could, from knowing how to handle an axe, do twice as much as I in half the time, with half the exertion, and he would be calm and smiling where I was sweating and puffing, striking every blow in a different place. After lunch we went up to the

Eagle River, and hailing the other side a man came across in a boat, or a vile apology for one, like the thing I had crossed the Illecilliwet in. However, we got across safely, and went farther up to another slough, and after working there awhile we left Williams at the job alone and came back to the river. Here Kyle told me he wanted to make a ferry, though he did not explain how he was going to do it. We had brought out with us in the morning two coils of rope, which he had left in the boat. When we got to the river again, to where this punt was, a quarter of a mile above where the railroad was to cross, we got in and I took the oars. As we drifted down Kyle told me what to do. There was just above the railroad crossing a long dead tree, bare of branches, lying on the bank, projecting half way over the stream, which is narrow but extremely rapid, running at least eight miles an hour. I was to let the boat drift right under the point of this tree, so that Kyle could throw a running noose over the end of it, which, as he stood up, would be four or five feet above his head. So down we swept, quicker and quicker, until at last we were right under it. Kyle threw and missed. 'Pull, pull, G— d— it, can't you pull?' he said. I swore back, 'Can't you see I am pulling?' But it was no use. I could not make any headway, strain as I might, with a flat-bowed thing against which the waters stood up. So down we went, and I had to pull to the shore nearest our camp. Then Kyle took the rope, when he had recovered from his fit of irritation, and walked out on the tree and put the loop on and came back again. My heart was in my mouth, for if he had slipped he would have had a hard struggle to save himself. However, he came to the bank in safety. Then he brought the rope down to the boat, and, holding on to it, we swung out into mid stream, and then tried to steer her over to the other side. We found it impossible to make the shore without letting the rope go, and then it would have been a great chance. So back we went, and Kyle pulled his watch out and said, ' It's past four now, and I promised to see someone in town at five. I must go, and you must get over and bring Williams across.' 'Yes,' said I, ' but how the devil am I to do it?' 'I don't know,' said Kyle, and strode off. I sat down and laughed. He and I could not get across, and now I was to do it myself. Then I grew serious, for I could not see how it was to be done. I looked at the stream and the strong eddies, then at the boat and the rude oars or paddles, then at the tree and the rope. I thought it impossible, and was very nearly turning round and walking off without even attempting it. However, I hit on a plan at last. I thought I could try at any rate, and if I was drowned it would be Kyle's fault, and I would, if possible, haunt him. My greatest fear, however, was not of drowning but of being carried down the river, which would deprive the men working there of all means of crossing at the old place. As I sat down, making plans, one of these men came to the opposite bank and asked how their boat got there, and when I told him he made some uncomplimentary remarks about Kyle. I asked him how I was to get across, and he said I couldn't do it. 'Well, I've got to do it.' 'Well, you can't,' and he disappeared. Then I got into the boat, laid hold of the rope, the loose end of which I tied to a stump, and hauled myself slowly up stream, hand over hand, until I was right under the tree again, and the water boiled in over the bows. I let go, jumped to the seat, snatched the oars, was caught in an eddy, and came just where I wanted to. So far so good; but the question now was how Williams and I were to get back again. If I had been able to bring the loose end of the rope over it would have been all right, but that had been impossible owing to its being too short. To start from that side without any rope, just in that place, would have taken us and boat probably a mile down stream. So there was nothing for it but to take the boat back to the place Kyle had brought it from, and a delightful task that proved. The banks were thick with brush, and trees projected over the water everywhere. One of the railroad men got in and tied a rope to the bows, and Williams and another hauled it up while I scrambled round the brush to pass the end on when they came to an impassable place Three times I fell in, once I had to swim and once I was dragged out by the scruff of the neck, before we got it back, and many were the curses levelled at my boss for his 'darned ingenuity' as the man in the boat called it. At last Williams and I got across, and set off just at dusk to walk eight miles or more to town, thinking that we had at any rate got over the worst and that the rest was plain sailing or plain walking. But we were greatly deceived. As we walked down the embankment of soft sand in the middle of the cedar forest the sky rapidly darkened and the wind came down in heavy puffs, like the forerunner of a gale. Up to this time I had not seen it blow much in British Columbia, except for a little while once at New Westminster, so I thought it would blow over and be nothing of consequence; but, instead of doing that, it came down heavier and heavier, until it ceased puffing and came in violent blasts, each lasting longer than the other, and fairly screaming in the trees. Then needles and dead branches began to fly, and presently a tree crashed down and then another. We had got by this time to a long slough with a log-bridge lying in the water across it, and on both sides there were parties of men at work. We saw them standing up on the grade looking round, and then one made a run and then another, trying to find a better place. Then the gale's force suddenly increased, and a dozen cedars came down at once all round us, with a roar like thunder, and all through the thick timber they fell right and left, one lodging against another, then both would go. And the fires lighted by the men to make their supper roared and crackled in the wind, sending out clouds of sparks and red embers. And the rain began to fall heavily, blown stingingly right in one's face. I ran out into the middle of the slough on to the bridge, thinking it might be safer, but when out there the tall trees seemed to bend over to me, and I ran right across to where the others were scuttling round like holeless rabbits, trying to find a shelter.

And meantime there was a perfect windy pandemonium in the forest, roars and shrieks of wind, and crash, crash, crash came more trees, here, there, and everywhere, some into the slough, some across the grade near where we were standing, and others in the distance; the rain was piercing and stinging, and sparks flew into the forest and set fire to the brush, and were extinguished again and again.

Finally, after about an hour, it began to lull, and came less and less, and no more trees fell. Presently Williams came across the slough and we made a fresh start home, and after a weary tramp in the rain got to the store. I went in. 'Hallo,' said Requa, 'you look like a ghost, or as if you had seen one.' Mr. Kyle was sitting near. 'Mr. Kyle,' said I, 'I brought Williams over, but you let me in for a nice thing. We had to drag that boat up stream and I fell in three times, and afterwards we nearly came to an end on the grade with the wind. Trees are lying all over the work.' He was grinning till I came to the last, but that touched him a little, for he was in a great hurry to get the job finished, and anything likely to delay it made him wild. So he stopped his smile and said, 'Very well, that will do; I'll go up to-morrow.' They had had it nearly as bad in town, and there had been a big waterspout on the lake. The amount of fallen timber must have been immense, and that so much of it fell was owing to a fire that had been through the forest the year before, which had burnt round the butts of the trees and weakened them.

Soon after this came the Fourth of July, which, strange to say, was kept with games and rejoicings and fights and much intoxication, just as if it had been on American or United States soil. We had a horse-race down the narrow street, and jumping, throwing the hammer and tossing the caber. In the afternoon came running and an incidental fight, because our brawny blacksmith kicked a dog out of the way of the runners. 'Don't you do that,' said the owner. 'I'll kick you off too.' 'Will you?' No sooner was he dared than the blacksmith knocked his opponent down and kicked him just over the eye. Then the constable interfered and got a blow in the mouth. There was every prospect of a general *mêlée*, but things quieted down and the games went on, and at last we had a tug of war, in which I was picked on one side. I confess our side was beaten, however, and the others drank the keg of beer, which was the prize. By this time it was dark, and at least 75 per cent. of the population were drunk and vociferous, and there was great howling down the street all night, and lugubrious procession of black eyes and swollen heads next day.

In the middle of the month I had a trip down to Kamloops on a very unpleasant errand, for Kyle sent me there with some others in charge of the body of a young fellow who had been killed in his tent one night by a tree falling on him when asleep. I had to go to the funeral, and was glad enough to get back to the pass again to my horses and novel reading in the hay.

I read a good deal of trash this time, and only remember Hardy's 'Far from the Madding Crowd,' the best novel I had seen then for many a long day. And then I got Meredith's ' Diana of the Crossways,' and the first volume of Ruskin's ' Stones of Venice,' and became temporarily learned in voussoirs, spandrels, arches, ornaments, &c.

During this month we had still a very lively time in town, with occasional intervals of comparative quiet for a day or two when Mr. Todd, the magistrate, came up from Kamloops, for then the unlicensed liquor dealers would hold their hands and go quietly, so that no one could be very drunk in town. One day he came into our store, when it was fearfully warm, and sat down sighing. 'Don't you find it rather dull here, Mr. Todd?' said I. 'It is a little dull after Kamloops.' 'Well,' said I, smiling, 'you can bet your life it will be livelier when you leave town.' He smiled himself, rather feebly, and left me sewing sacks, to keep myself from dying of *ennui* and heat combined.

When I look back on those months they were really very happy. I had not too much to do; I was saving nearly ten pounds a month; I had novels and my two classical dead friends, and my unclassical live friend Scott, who would come in and argue about religion, and get me to tell him something about Darwin, in order that he might try to controvert what I said. Then there was our daily swimming, canoeing in Indian canoes, and jabbering with Indians, and rowing over to Major Rogers's place at Sickamoose Narrows. And good board was to be had, even in this place. Better than all, I did not suffer from home sickness, which can so unaccountably destroy all pleasure in life at times.

And then I actually had a long conversation with another educated man, a Church of England clergyman, from Kamloops, who had come up to do a little preaching to those who would listen. And these were few. I took care of his horse, and so got acquainted with him, and one night he came down to the stable to see the animal, and then we sat down on the edge of a boat—Taffy's boat, by the way—and argued of strange things, 'free will, fixed fate, foreknowledge absolute,' and the 'origin of evil,' and finding that the discussion would be interminable for lack of something we could really agree upon, we went off into English literature, having a pleasant talk about many different authors. Then I told him about my meeting the two clergymen in the Fraser Cañon, and made him laugh about the pie, although his knowledge of cooking was no greater than Mr. Edwards's, the author of that most abominable crust.

So altogether I did not spend those three months to any great disadvantage, and I was sorry enough when Mr. Kyle told me he would not require my services any longer, as there was so little to do. I had been expecting this for some time, as during the last two weeks I was with him I did not do a good day's work. So I took my money, bade farewell to Eagle Pass Landing, went on board the 'Peerless,' and back to Kamloops.

CHAPTER XVI.

TO VANCOUVER ISLAND AND VICTORIA.

In Kamloops I sent home 100 dols., leaving myself about 40 dols., thinking that would be sufficient to see me through a period of rest, but I was sorry before long that I had not kept it, as will be seen.

I went over to Hughes's, and stayed there a few days, doing a few odd jobs for him, and hunted a little and fished. I met an old acquaintance there again, an Indian woman, Mary, who had been married to a white man near Kamloops, who nearly killed her with a shovel. So she left him, and when I knew her was living with an American from Maine, who certainly did not try to kill her, but still used to beat her. They would go into town together and get drunk, and then fight and squabble. I got her to make me a pair of moccasins, which I lost going down to the coast. I had a pleasant week at Hughes's place, not doing more work than made me fit to eat a good dinner, and we had great talks and discussions, making plans of meeting one day in London, which may yet come to pass. Then at last, getting tired of doing nothing and earning nothing, I thought I would go to the coast again.

So I bade my friend Mr. Hughes farewell, and off I went to Savona. I found an old saw-mill friend at Van Horne, a man who was half an Indian by dint of living with them, who could talk Chinook as fluently as English, and with him I started to walk down once more, firmly determined not to pay the exorbitant railroad fare; and I walked the whole way to Yale again, looking in at my friends the clergymen's place near Jackass Mountain, of course, as I passed by. They gave us dinner, and we stayed to service with a crowd of Indians, and heard them talk to them in a strange soft tongue, very different from the guttural language of the coast.

Then to Yale, and thence by steamer to New Westminster, and the Farmers' Home.

I had been so careless of money coming down that I found I was running short once more, as usual with me, and as the mill had 'started up' on a different basis I went to work there again, but had trouble with another Chinaman, and was discharged for knocking him down. This was the second time. It was very unfortunate.

I had only about 10 dols. If I had had four times as much I should have bought a rifle and hunted and trapped that winter, but under the circumstances I thought it best to leave British Columbia, especially as I was told the Chinaman was going to take me to court, and I should have been heavily fined if he had. Of course I could have got help to pay it if it had come to that, but I thought it best to avoid accidents, so I jumped on board the 'Teaser' for Victoria. The last incident of note in New Westminster was my meeting with a Japanese sailor, who had been looking on in the mill when I had the difficulty with the Mongolian, and who insisted on shaking hands with me for thrashing him; for these Japanese cordially hate their neighbours, and regard them, as this one and many another told me, as 'pigs and dogs.'

We ran down out of the river and were in the Straits of Georgia, on the sea. Not the open sea, for it looked more like a large lake, yet it had the smell of the brine and the long roll of the sea, and the seaweed, and it was pleasant to me, whose last sight of open salt water had been outside of Sandy Hook. We ran across the straits, down a multiplicity of channels, among a thousand islands wooded to the very edge of the water, and came at last into the land-locked, pleasant little harbour of Victoria.

I had by this time picked up a companion or partner on board. He was an Englishman who had been in the Cape Mounted Rifles and the Mounted Police of the North-West Provinces east of the Rockies, from which he had been discharged as an invalid. He was a tall, strange individual, in a sort of velveteen jacket, evidently a gentleman, and with a good voice and English accent, but there was something uncanny about him. One might suspect him of being haunted. We talked a great deal of British Columbia, and I found he had been at Hughes's once. Then I remembered Hughes had told me of such a one who came and asked for work during haying time, and when terms were agreed upon said he would like to go and read the newspaper that afternoon, and, finally, that he thought he would not work there, but would try to get a job that would last longer somewhere else. I found out he was the same individual. He had since then been at the Spullamacheen Valley and was going to Victoria to try to get admission to the hospital.

In Victoria I went to the same hotel, and slept in the same room with him, and was rather alarmed at the wild way he talked. He was clearly insane. He raved about his relatives in England who had robbed him of his money, of his comrades in the Mounted Police who had put forth evil reports about him, and even about the people in Victoria, who knew what had been said of him, for he had heard them talking about him in the streets. I went to sleep, but not without some misgivings, glad that he had no razor in his valise, for he looked no unlikely subject for homicidal mania.

Next day I was relieved by his getting admission to the hospital, which, unless I am much mistaken, would be a first step to his obtaining a permanent refuge at the lunatic asylum, certainly the best place for him.

I was now coming down gradually in cash, and was in a very fair way to have nothing at all. It really seemed to me that it was my fate to be perpetually in financial difficulties, for no sooner did I get anything than it vanished again, and when I got a good job it would not last. But then a bad one would not either. I was perpetually in anxiety, and sometimes even felt inclined to spend my last dollar or two recklessly, in order to know the worst at once and be no more in suspense. As I was walking about town in a state of mental inquiry as to ways and means, occasionally asking for work at some likely-looking place, I met suddenly my two friends from the cañon. Now I was a pretty object to talk to clergymen in a populous city. It is true my old Texas hat had been discarded at Eagle Pass, but I was nevertheless only in rough working clothes, and doubtless the state of my pocket might have been discerned by a keen observer in my dejected face. Nevertheless my wild appearance did not daunt Mr. Small and Mr. Edwardes, who bore down with smiling faces and shook hands, making all sorts of inquiries. Then I walked down the street with them, feeling something like a prisoner between two policemen, and many were the curious glances cast at me by passers-by when they saw me in such company. Perhaps they thought I was a brand snatched from the burning.

I met a man from the hotel in which I was staying, and his astonishment and temporary paralysis were delightful, and I had to stand a considerable amount of chaff about my 'high-toned' acquaintances when I left them, after promising to lunch with them next day. I tried to get off, but they insisted, so I went to a good restaurant with them, and surprised the waiter, who at first, I have no doubt, thought I was an unfortunate man these two charitable individuals had brought in to save from starvation; but when he saw the terms we were on, and heard snatches of our conversation, he looked at me with more respect and a great amount of subdued curiosity. After lunch we went out and hired a boat, and I pulled them round to Esquimault Harbour, and we took a look at H.M.S. 'Triumph.' Coming back we got into a religious argument, and I fear they got to look at me as a very heathen, for my views and pessimistic philosophy of life seemed, no doubt, extremely wrong viewed from their standpoint, and it was with the sorrowful charity of shocked yet forgiving spirits that they parted from me for the last time. And I was left alone to come back from metaphysics to the reality I philosophically denied, and from subjective introspective analysis of motives impelling to action, faith, or belief, to the objectivity of nearly penniless pockets and need of paid employment.

That afternoon I went down to the wharves and asked the mate of the steamer 'Olympian,' which ran down the Sound, to let me work my way to Tacoma, and after several refusals, as I refused to be denied, he told me to take a truck, and I helped discharge her cargo and then to load her up again, working like a horse, running and sweating along with the regular hands.

So I left Victoria and ran down Puget Sound, calling in at Port Townsend, Port Ludlow, Port Madison, and Seattle, doing little or nothing on the way down, as there was no discharging to do until I came in the morning to Tacoma.

CHAPTER XVII.

MOUNT TACOMA OVERHEAD.

As I had had breakfast on board the steamer, I was not obliged to pay out anything from my scanty stock for meals, and I went up town to look for work. I soon discovered that I had jumped out of the frying-pan into the fire, and there was even less to be done in Tacoma than in Victoria. I tried road contractors and house builders, but could not even get work at mixing mortar. I went to the coal wharves and tried to obtain employment trimming coal, but every one was full handed. Then I walked down to the great saw-mill, and tackled every one about the place without success, until at last I came to the man who superintended the loading of the vessels at the mill's wharves. Yes, I could come down in the afternoon and go to work. Then I wanted to know the wages. He looked at me. 'Oh, it's the wages you want to know! Then you can wait till you find out.' I got wild and 'talked back,' and finally told him and the mill to go to a warm locality, for I didn't want his work, and wouldn't work under him at any price. This, of course, was not true; but then I had never been answered in that way in all my life, and it very naturally made me angry. And the fact that he answered in such a way showed me that men must be very plentiful, or he would not have ventured to speak so, for the bosses are polite enough when hands are scarce. I walked off boiling, and made up my mind to leave Tacoma and the Sound and go to Portland. Then I would go to sea again and get out of America. I began to think I had had enough of it.

I walked up town, and, in order to reduce myself to a cool and quiet state of mind, I climbed the hills beyond the main street, for I desired to see Mount Tacoma, which I had been told was a lofty and magnificent mountain. After a while I turned and looked back, but could see nothing, for all the level land across the head of the Sound was filled with a mass of vapour. I sat down and waited, and presently mist and cloud began to shift and roll in the wind, that bared to me at last the most glorious mountain I had yet seen. The peaks of the Rockies faded from my memory, and the snowy pinnacles of the Selkirks—even the white cone of Mount Baker—were hidden and diminished, as this white miracle of rock and ice and snow rose before me, towering nearly fifteen thousand feet above the sea that was at my feet and the level lands at its base. Its tremendous majesty is not lessened by division of peaks nor marred by additions; it is one and indivisible, solitary, patriarchal yet childless. It lifts its ancient head for ever above the clouds; the storm thunder rolls below the thunder of its loosening avalanches; the scream of the soaring eagle fails to pierce to the olden silence of that height; and only the fires of the stars are above the cold sharp jewels of its glittering icy crest; only the splendour of the sun can kindle it to responsive rose, that magic colour beyond even the ethereal glory of the rainbow and the tinged fleece of floating clouds at even. It is imperial, antique, beyond worship, eternal and godlike.

I had seen a mountain, and one unsurpassed in Alps and Andes. Is there a greater on Himalay?

I came back slowly to earth after that, not this time from the depths of subjectivity but from the rapt state of ecstasy that one knows so seldom, when one becomes one with Nature for a while, and an unreasoning pantheist, when one's eyes are blind to anything but the glory of the universe, and one's ears are deaf to the anguish of the world, and forgetful even of one's own. I was alone that hour, and I am glad; a voice would have jarred on me like a false note in an exquisite sonata, and even another silent like myself would have kept me to the earth and reality. For that time I was a mystic, a theopath, and a believer in dreams and visions, and the mountain was alive, theurgic, whole and part of me, and the sea-strait beneath and the sky above were ways for spirits and spiritual ministering, and sacred.

Yet I came back to reality, pain, anxiety, to converse with brutish men, and weariness of the flesh.

My plan was now to get out of this town and go to Portland, that was now so near to me, in comparison with the huge distance when I had dreamed of a raft voyage down the Columbia from the Rocky Mountains. As it was impossible for me to pay my fare, since I had but two dollars and a half, there remained two courses open to me. I could walk or 'beat my way' on the train. I declined walking; I had had enough of it in British Columbia, toiling to and fro over mountain and road, so there remained but 'beating.' I had to find a freight or goods train, and in it an open or unlocked car in which I could secrete myself, so that I might be taken to Portland without any one knowing. And even if I was found out perhaps a dollar would set it right with the conductor or brakesman, who are, as a rule, not above making an addition to their pay. So I went down to the railroad yards, and was told by a man to go to a certain hotel, kept by an ex-conductor, who would be able to put me up to the tricks and tell me what train would be best for me to take. I went there, and found out that there was a train at four o'clock next morning going to Portland. I learnt the conductor's name, but was told to keep out of his way. I could find out nothing about the brakesman.

I went down in the evening to the place from which the train would start, near which there was a sawmill, and I soon made friends with the night watchman, who promised to find me a good pile of sawdust to sleep on, which would save me paying for a bed, which I could as ill afford as when I was in Chicago. I sat down by the fire and talked and smoked with him till ten o'clock, and then together we hunted up some good shavings and sawdust, and I spread my blankets out and went to sleep most placidly.

Next morning, at half-past three, he called me, and I rolled up my blankets and went out into the darkness to seek my train, after shaking hands with him. When I came to the cars I went along trying the doors, and was nearly caught by the conductor. However, I hid in some lumber until he passed by, and then came out again, finding, fortunately, a car with the end door open. I jumped up, put my head in, and finding there was room I dropped my blankets inside, following them as quickly as possible, shutting the door behind me. I found there was very little stuff in the car, but making my way nearly to the other end I kicked a soft yielding mass, which grunted out: 'Hallo, partner, where are you coming to?' 'Didn't see you, pard, it's too dark,' said I; and then thinking I had heard the voice before, asked: 'Ain't you the Irishman I spoke to last night?' 'Yes, I am.' So we knew each other, and presently, when the engine whistled and rang her bell, and started out, I lighted a match and took a look at my companion and my travelling carriage, or 'side-door Pullman,' as the 'tramps' and 'dead-beats' facetiously call them. It was new and smelt most villanously of vile paint, there were some planks in it, dirty and evil, the floor had cracks in it, and the sides as well. My Irish friend was a man about thirty-five or forty, or even more, bearded and dirty, with a longish upper lip and a sulky inward look—in all respects a man whom I did not desire as a companion or a friend. He was lying down with his head on his blankets, chewing tobacco. I spread mine out and rolled myself up in them, and soon went to sleep, waking up every time the train stopped. About two hours from the time of starting, when we were side-tracked, waiting for a train to pass us on the single line, the door was suddenly shot back on its slide and a young fellow leapt in. 'Hallo, you fellows, where are you bound for?' 'Portland,' said I, sitting up and biting off a bit of tobacco to show I was at my ease. 'Well, you'll have to put up the stuff (*Anglicè*, put down some money), or you can't travel.' 'How much will do it?' said my Irish partner. 'A dollar and a half each.' We both swore it couldn't be done. 'I haven't got a dollar and a half,' I said. I lied. I had 2.50 dols. Then he came down to a dollar and a quarter. 'Yes,' said I, 'but suppose we give you the cash now, what will happen if the conductor comes along?' 'That will be all right.' 'No, it won't be all right, brakie; I know this man's name, it's M——, and you know it isn't all right.' This took him aback. 'Well, I'll tell you what I'll do. If you'll give me a dollar and a quarter after we get across the Columbia at Kalama I'll let you ride. If you get bounced by M—— before then it will be my loss, and if it's over the other side it will be yours.' 'That's a bargain,' said I; 'you shall have it when we cross.' So he went away, and I went to sleep again for a while, and then woke up and sat smoking and thinking about the stories my brother used to tell me about beating his way in New Mexico. Very often men will ride on the engine above the pilot or cow-catcher, and sometimes even inside it. Then some men travel on the passenger-trains, on top of the cars, or on the baggage-car at the end where there is no door—the 'blind baggage,' as it is called. And, besides this, there is what is known as the 'universal ticket,' a board with notches in it to fit on the iron stays under the passenger-coaches. Some, too, will ride on the brake-beam. In fact there is no method, however hazardous it may be, that is not practised by men who want to go somewhere in a hurry or without walking. My Irishman told me that he was travelling in Oregon once, and was standing up between the freight-cars, with his feet on the coupling, holding on to the steps with his hands. A brakesman coming along on top noticed him, and demanded a dollar, which the Irishman either wouldn't or couldn't pay. The brakie came down a step and made a kick at him. 'I grabbed hold of his leg,' said he, 'and held him. He couldn't let go with his hands or shift his other foot. It was a pretty position. But I got tired myself, and at last I sez: "Will you be quiet if I let yez go?" "I will," sez he, for he was scared I should pull him down and throw him under the wheels, and devil the good in his hollering for the row of the train. So I lets him up. And what do you think the murdering blagaird did? He goes right back to the caboose, I guess, and fetches a coupling-pin' (of iron, about one inch thick and ten inches long) 'and comes over me and sez: "Take that, you dam bum," and lets drive at me. When I see him lift his arm I pulled my six-shooter. The pin came down an' just missed me, an' I shot at him. Away he goes forward, and presently the train slackens up. Sez I: "It's time I left, if I don't want to be killed." So I jumps off, and rolls twenty feet down a bank. I scrambled on me hands and knees about twenty yards, for I was hurt, and I couldn't run, and got into a thick bush, an' I lay low. The fireman and brakie and the conductor came huntin' me with lanterns, and two o' them had guns, and I heard 'em swear to kill me. I cocks mine and says: "Not if I can help it." Twice that brakie came within five yards o' me, and each time I was just going to shoot him when he turned off. At last they gets tired, and goes on board the train, cursing horrible, you bet. I wish I'd killed the bastard anyhow.'

With such yarns we beguiled the time, and I began to think that we were going 'slick' through to Portland, but I reckoned without the conductor. When we stopped at a small station, after running about five hours, the door slid back again and a different head looked in. 'Hallo, boys, how are you making it?' with a sardonic grin that boded us no good. 'Oh, well enough,' said I. 'Are you going to Portland?' 'That's where I'm going.' 'Then you had better get out and walk.' I grinned and sat still. 'It's far easier this way. Ain't you going to let us ride?' 'Not by a darn sight. You've come ninety miles, and that's good enough.' 'Well,' said I at last, 'if I must I must,' and I grabbed my blankets and jumped out, thinking at any rate that I had saved my dollar and if the 'con' had found us on the other side the dollar and the ride would have both been lost. So I rolled up my loose blankets on a pile of ties, while the Irishman sat smoking alongside philosophically. I heard a colloquy between the brakie and the conductor. The former was angry with the latter for spoiling his little game, and the conductor evidently enjoyed the whole business. Finally he said : 'Who's running this train, you or I? If you don't like what I do you can get off and walk.' So the brakie 'dried up' and said no more. Presently the train moved off, and I found myself at Cowlitz, ten miles from the Columbia, and set out to walk, soon leaving the Irishman behind. After walking five miles, I heard a hand-car coming along behind me, with some section hands working it along by means of the lever, 'pumping,' as it is commonly called. When they came up with me the boss stopped it and invited me to take a ride and pump with them. So I was on a hand-car again, for the first time since I had left the section in Iowa, where Ray Kern and I worked for three days. In a very short time we ran into Kalama, and I went and got some supper and slept in a big deserted house that had been built when the town had a 'boom'—*i.e.* when there was great speculation in lots and building, and a great future was predicted for it. This is the place where the cars run across the river on a big ferry-boat; from the farther side they then go to Portland.

Next morning I went across with the passenger-train, paid a dollar to go to that town, and soon arrived there, an utter stranger with no friends and a dollar and a half in my pocket. This was just as usual, however, and by this time I began to get used to it, and did not feel as miserable as I ought to have done. I went to a cheap hotel, had supper, and next morning began to look for a ship to get out of America. I was not particular where I went—England, Australia, South America, or China.

I had a notion then in my head to go to China, thence to Singapore, thence to Calcutta, and then home to England through the Suez Canal; or I could go to Australia, and thence to Calcutta, in some of the ships that take Australian horses for mounting the Indian cavalry. I had been to sea before, indeed I had served as an 'able-bodied seaman' between England and Australia for a while, and though six or seven years had elapsed since my more youthful escapades, I thought I had still enough of the business at my fingers' ends to carry me through. So I walked down to the wharves along the Willammette (accented on the second syllable), and the first vessel I came to I was lucky enough to get a job in. This was a barque, the 'Coloma,' of Portland, bound to China with lumber and returning Chinamen. I spoke to the mate at the gangway as he was tallying lumber down the chute into the bow-ports, and afterwards to the skipper, presenting him with my brother's certificate of discharge, as I had lost my own by shipping once before in England for New Zealand in a fit of pique—a foolish love affair—and then backing out just before she sailed. I was told to come to work in the afternoon. I brought down my bundle, had dinner, and stowed lumber down in the hold with my new companions. It was hard work, lifting heavy planks, forty feet long, in a confined space, driving them in with a sledge-hammer or using another plank as a ram. Then sometimes lumber would come down without much warning, through the carelessness of the man on the look-out for it, and it was necessary then to jump for one's life, or at any rate to save one's legs.

My shipmates were a mixed lot. One was a

Frenchman from France, not a Canadian Frenchman, who spoke very bad English, so bad that I had to make him talk French slowly when I wanted to understand him particularly, but at other times I would let him ramble on unintelligibly, throwing in a few remarks at random to make him believe I was listening. Another was an old Englishman, formerly sailing in the steamers from England to the West Coast of Africa : a little man he was, whose boast was that he never got drunk, although he drank to excess. He told me many horrible and circumstantial accounts of fever-stricken ships, and how once he made canvas shrouds for eighteen men on the voyage home, the only survivors of passengers and crew being himself, the captain, two firemen, and an engineer. There was a Newcastle-on-Tyne man, a Geordie, fair and blue-eyed and strong and broad-shouldered, a gay Lothario of seamen, and a babbler concerning 'bonnes fortunes,' but a good-hearted, pleasant Englishman. After him, in my mind, comes an Irish sailor, long in America, lithe and loose-jointed, perpetually smiling, mirthful and mirth-provocative, loud and witty, a great joker, a natural humourist, a born low comedian out of his element. He made me laugh against my will, waking me in the dead of night by stumbling into the fo'cs'le half-drunk. His first remark in the dark would make laughter and sleep struggle against each other in me, and by the time he had the lamp lighted I would be shaking in my bunk and shouting.

Down below, working in the hold, it was the same; time 'could not stale, nor custom wither his infinite variety' of facial contortion and remarks. Once he nearly caused me to fall from aloft by making me laugh until my sides ached.

He was delightful so, and at the same time an inimitable *raconteur*. Three times had ships sailing from the Pacific coast to England foundered, compelling him and the rest of the crew to the boats, after laborious pumping day and night, until some died of fatigue and some jumped overboard.

Then in the West Indies, one time, the cook died of yellow jack, and the captain made him cook, much against his will. He got on well enough for a while, cooking beef and potatoes, as the bread came from the shore. But one day the skipper brought ten pounds of rice on board, and told him they would have rice for dinner that day in the cabin. Now Jim knew as much about rice as a man would who had only eaten it, and thinking, from the size of the bag, that it would about do for the three in the cabin, leaving perhaps some for himself, he began to cook the whole of it. His account of the progress of that cooking was delightful: how it swelled up and thrust the lid off, and began to pour out on the range; how he snatched more saucepans, and how those filled up and came over; and how, finally, every available pot he had was choking with rice, while he was ladling it out, blind with excitement, on to a board. His tragic accents and facial play would have made his fortune as a story-teller.

At night time he and Geordie and I went up town, but after a little while I always left them, to avoid getting drunk, as both of them could drink buckets of lager beer, while five glasses would be more than enough for me; indeed, four would make me crawl along the gang-plank to the t'gallant fo'cs'le for safety. Then they would come in, boisterous and singing, at midnight.

Our officers were mixed, as usual. The captain was very quiet, and, as far as I found him, very considerate.

The chief officer, or first mate, was a big, heavy man, weighing about fifteen stone, loud-voiced but good-tempered, and yet rather a dangerous man to handle, I fancy. At any rate, I had no desire to try conclusions with him. The second mate was my particular aversion, and it was through him I left the ship. I had soon found out, when once on board, that as my sea-education had been very hasty I had forgotten a great part of it after six years of the land, and that made this second mate take a dislike to me. Then he had a particularly bullying way of speaking to all of us, and I disliked it very much. He used to look at me sometimes as if he was saying, 'Wait till I get you to sea.' Now I could have whipped him if it had only been between us two, but I knew that if I had trouble with him at sea I should have to reckon with the mate as well, and I could not have whipped him And, to make things worse, one day the second mate set me to grease down the mizzentopmast, and would not give me a bo'son's chair. I refused to do it, and the ensuing altercation was heard by the captain, who ordered him to give me one, saying I could not be expected to do it without. This made him thoroughly my enemy. So, after I had been on board two weeks, I determined to leave, although I had signed articles, and having got my money due for working with lumber, which was paid every Saturday night, and a little more of that due to me from the monthly wages on the pretext of wanting to buy some underclothing, I left her early on Monday morning with my blankets and five dollars cash, intending to see if I could not get work in the country in the valley of the Willammette. And if I was unsuccessful I could walk south towards California, keeping in my mind, as an ultimate possible destination, the city of San Francisco.

CHAPTER XVIII.

OREGON UNDERFOOT.

ALL Oregon was before me where to choose, and I determined on that southward course. I was sorry indeed to feel myself forced to leave the 'Coloma,' but still I knew it was probable I should have come to Hong Kong in irons, or maybe not at all, for the occasional brutality of American officers is incredible, and far beyond anything that occurs in English ships. So I cast loose and let myself into the stream of Destiny, that runs for ever southward to that 'common sink,' San Francisco; whither, sooner or later, all men on the Pacific slope must come for awhile, drawn by the magnetic influence of a great city.

Portland, that flourishing, detestable, Chinese-ridden town, that selfish city, I left without regret. Here they believe that the part is greater than the whole, that their prosperity overweighs calamity even of greater Oregon, and that all the rest was made for them.

So my time in America had not come to an end, and the 'terminus ad quem' was unknown and unknowable. I was thrown back again on myself, and my late companions were behind me and a cloud-covered path before me.

I went over the river and took a ticket for Aurora, so that I should get a good start into the country far from the city, as the farther I went the more likelihood there would, be in all probability, of obtaining work. And when Aurora came I sat still in the cars, in order that I might go a little farther without paying for it. If the conductor had not come to me I would have gone on as far as the train went, but he politely reminded me that my ticket had been for Aurora; so I had to get out at Hubbard, and walked down the line after the disappearing train.

I felt most melancholy for the rest of that day, and my thoughts ranged forward without finding any satisfaction, and backwards with regret. It seemed as if I had no will of my own; that I was but the sport of Necessity and Destiny—a straw on a stream to be carried on or lodged on a bar, as it might be. The sky of blue was dull, and the singing of birds melancholy, and the wind a dirge and a wail. I was too much alone, and dwelt in a cave without light; no natural cave-dweller or troglodyte, but a prisoner with all natural friendly impulses and affections repulsed and rejected. Like a vine that finds no support for its tendrils to grow on and to be uplifted by, I ran along the ground, thrown down. My sacrifices were rejected, my fires quenched, and the heavy smoke ran low in the air, portending storm. I was raging, nihilistic, anarchist, a mutineer against gods and men, a sneerer, a scoffer, atheist even as to Nature and Loveliness; a misanthrope, a misogynist, a reviler of all things, a Sadducee, a Philistine. For the iron entered my soul. And I walked like a whirlwind, with a pestilence and despair in me, self-contained and wrathful. I ate in silence or went hungry in silence. I rose up in starvation, and lived on apple orchards like a bird of prey forced to hateful fruits, lacking blood and flesh. I passed men on the road and spoke not. If they spoke to me I did but stare at them, and went by in strange quiet. This for days. Then I came back to myself somewhat, yet still walking as if towards a fixed goal that was far off. I asked for work and asked in vain; there was no work and no money, and the hospitality was niggard and mean and unbountiful. I was no happy tramp who never worked, preferring to beg and lie in the sun or steal; I was strong and tall, and could do most things; yet no work. I passed quiet Salem and widespread Albany, and through Eugene City without hope. At night I camped out without supper; in the morning I awoke cold and chilled through, and walked in hunger. I bought but little, and got a meal now and again for chopping wood. I split much during that journey, oak and pine, madrona and manzanita. I drove the axe down vengefully, as though an enemy's head was beneath the keen edge.

I filed saws for people. I did all things that came to hand; but no work yet to be obtained.

And I left the fruitful, cursed Willammette Valley, and strove across the range to the valley of the North Umpqua River, walking, recklessly and hard, nearly forty miles that day. And that night found a human being on the range, a farmer and a man, who spoke kindly and asked me in. I remember him gratefully. Then through Oakland, old and new, and across the North Umpqua River to Roseberg. Still no work, and starvation. And I left the road, crossed the South Umpqua, wading it, and went up Rice Creek into the hills, meeting no work but more friendly people. Then to Olallie Creek, for I heard of rail-splitting to be had. I came to a little house belonging to some men owning sheep. My hope proved vain. They had nothing to do. That night I slept a mile away down in the quiet valley, getting breakfast in the morning. And then the trail to Cow Creek, and to Riddle. This was a pleasant walk, and I began to recover from my fit of depression. The air was bright and kind and large. I could breathe. And as I went along the ridges of the hills I looked down on peace and solitude, and sunlight and shadow. And ever and again, as I walked quietly along the unfrequented trail, a deer would jump through the brush and plunge leaping down or up the hill. And I sat down and took out my Virgil and read part of the Sixth Book, and got up calmer and better than I had been for days. I had come up from the Avernus for a while.

I came at last out of the trail on to a road and a little house on the side of the hill. Beneath lay a stretch of plain with farmed land and houses, and beyond a line of willowy creek, and beyond again hills. Under the verandah of the house sat a man reading. I went up and said 'Good day,' which he pleasantly returned. I saw I had come across no ordinary farmer. He was an educated man evidently, with good forehead and head and keen eyes, though spectacled. His hands were finely shaped, though hard and brown as his face; good teeth and supple lips, and a fine smile; young, about thirty-five perhaps. I sat down beside him. Presently he gave me the paper, and I sat down and read the news. I asked him for a bit of tobacco, and he gave me nearly half a pound. Then he asked me to stay for dinner, and introduced me to his wife, a gentle, pleasant, girlish, graceful figure, with much intelligence if slightly uncultured. Her pet fawn, with large ears and lovely eyes, made friends with me. After dinner we sat and talked. He was manager of a mine near at hand, an assayer and practical miner, a chemist too. He took me to his little laboratory, and I showed him that I remembered a little of the chemistry I had learnt in days gone by, and mentioned some of the best known names in that science. Then we spoke of books, and I found him well informed even outside of his specialty. So I spent a pleasant hour or two, and parted with him regretfully.

I came down to Cow Creek, and passed on to Canyonville, sleeping in the cañon in a barn that night, walking next morning fifteen miles before I got breakfast. Then I ran into the wilderness again of Wolf Creek, and spent 25 cents of the last little money I had in buying a can of salmon, which I devoured sitting on a log in the forest, and came at night to Grave Creek, and split a pile of oakwood, getting a good supper thereby and a long talk with the hired girl, who was pretty and pleasant, not deeming me a common tramp.

Then onward next day as hard as ever. And I came past Grant's Pass and saw Rogue River in the rain, and sat in a deserted barn, thinking what a fool I was to be there, while the rain came to sleet and snow, and the wind was bitter. Then to Woodville, and 25 cents gone for supper, and sleep in a barn, and no breakfast. And I came now to an old English farmer's place, still asking for work, and still finding there were more men in the country than were enough to do what was wanted. Then I saw the Rogue River Valley, beautiful, level to the base of the frowning Siskyou Mountains of Northern California, that lifted peak on peak of snow above that smiling valley. I walked miles through it in vain, and turned at last to Jacksonville, having then but one dollar.

I recklessly had supper and a bed that night. I had come 300 miles from Portland in twelve days.

Next morning I breakfasted with an old farmer, with whom I talked, telling him my adventures. He was a tall, thin, careful-looking individual, shaven. He said but little, but at last asked me whether I would go to work for 10 dols. a month. I would have willingly worked for nothing for a week or two, just to take a rest and be sure of my meals and a place to sleep. Indeed, I offered to work for the men on Olallie Creek for three days for nothing on that account. So I jumped at the offer. He said he lived near Waldo, sixty-five miles away, and that he was not going back for three days. He offered, rather unwillingly as I thought, to pay for my board in town until then, but I said no, that I would walk there, for I didn't want him to think that I was one of the very numerous class of men who would suddenly disappear at the end of the three days. So he gave me his name and directions, and I set out, having, when I had settled my bill at the hotel, thirty-five cents left to carry me sixty-five miles. However, I had served a good apprenticeship to starvation, and did not doubt my ability to walk the whole distance on nothing, since I was sure of a meal at the end. So I left Jacksonville with a lighter heart than I had since leaving Portland behind me. That day I walked steadily about twenty-five miles, having nothing to eat but a pound of dry biscuits.

I slept in a barn. Next day I started without breakfast, until I came to a farm at ten o'clock, where I got a meal for my last twenty-five cents. The country received but little attention from me, though it was worth more, as it was a gold-mining district. I passed the Applegate River, and many places where they were sluicing away the gravel with water, 'hydraulicking' as they call it, filling up the river with 'slickens' or soft mud. I walked all day with some degree of hunger, and slept in a barn, by this time ravenous. Next morning no breakfast, for I would not ask for it, as I knew I could get to my destination that day. I walked through Kirbyville, and then went out of my way. I was put right by two men, who asked me where I was going. When I told them they looked at me with pity : 'You are going to work for the meanest man in all Oregon.' This was consolatory, but I answered I was ready to work for the very devil himself sooner than work for nobody at all, and walk and starve.

Then I got lost again, and went nearly ten miles out of my way, for this place was so full of roads in every direction that it was impossible for a stranger to keep right. At last, by dint of inquiry, I made my way to what I imagined was the house. On one side of the road were barns and stables surrounded by a fence, and behind, forest and hills ; on the other stood a ramshackle old house, dirty outside, unpainted, with moss-green roof, with piles of rags and old boots on the verandah, and more rags stuffed in the broken and uncleaned windows. . It was antique but unvenerable, ruinous but not majestic. It looked like a miser's house. I went through a little badly hung gate, that was pulled to again by a string with an old saucepan hung to it for a weight, and went up to the door. H——, my boss, had told me there was a man named Pete working for him. I knocked, and getting no answer turned the handle. The inside was worse than the outside. I shut the door, and going to the back of the house saw somebody working in the orchard. I crossed the fence and went to him and said, 'Are you Pete?' 'Yes,' he said. 'Then, for God's sake, come and get me some dinner. H—— sent me out to work here, and I haven't had anything to eat since yesterday at eleven in the morning.' It was then three in the afternoon. Pete grinned and left his potato digging. He was a fine young fellow, keen-eyed and intelligent, with the figure of a man who has worked hard, but no harder than is sufficient to bring out all his strength ; his skin was beautiful and his eyes bright blue. He was confident, rather selfish, very self-reliant ; a man to get on in life if it could be done.

He made me some tea and cooked bacon, bringing out good bread, meanwhile talking about H——. This man had formerly been a lay preacher, through some extraordinary want of knowledge of his own character. He even then used to swear volubly, much to Pete's astonishment when a child, as he averred. Then he gave up what he had no vocation for, and turned all his attention to farming and money making. Pete prophesied evil times for me, but told me to stand no nonsense and talk back if necessary. This I felt quite able to do, and generally I thought myself able to 'hold up my end' in a row.

Pete and I spent all next day together digging potatoes and making fences, and in the evening H—— came home. Pete stayed three days more and then left. So I was left alone with my 'meanest man in Southern Oregon.' I did not find him very difficult to get along with however, for I worked hard, and if he growled in spite of what I did I growled back. The weather was very bad, raining nearly all the time, but I lost scarcely an hour through that. I had four to six horses to look after and the stable to clean. I fed these and about twenty head of cows and calves. I did what milking was to be done. I chopped the wood, got up in the morning to light the fire, and often cooked the breakfast. Then we hauled firewood and made fences. I rode for letters and after cattle. I did everything, and he did nothing at all at first, for his hand was but then recovering from a felon or whitlow. Pete told me that a man who had been there before me had had a very bad hand with the same disease, and that H—— had charged him four dols. a week for his board, and made him as uncomfortable as he could, jeering at his sufferings.

Then he got one himself, and behaved like a sick child.

One day, when I came in from the field, I found H——'s brother Angus was in the house. He had come from Crescent City, in Del Norte County, California, having been further south, working in the redwoods of Mendocino County. A greater difference could not be between two brothers. Angus was fifteen years younger, stout and ruddy, with a full beard and an open, pleasant smile. He had the greatest contempt in some ways for the other, declaring that all the meanness of the whole family had centred in him. His coming was a great relief to me; I had someone to talk to; and then, as Angus worked there and I with him, he would quit work before I could have done had I been alone. Then if H—— ever growled he would take up the cudgels for me as I sat silent smoking by the fire. Then he did all the cooking, which not only resulted in greater freedom for me, but in better bread and food, though there were great rows at intervals between the brothers about the tea, as the elder liked it weak and the younger strong.

All this time I did various kinds of work, sometimes harrowing with three horses, sometimes hauling rails. And then all three of us went out felling timber, and we hewed out logs to build a place to put roots and potatoes in, using axe and broad axe, 'weapon naked, shapely, wan,' as Walt Whitman calls it.

S

On Sundays I would take the rifle and go hunting, not so much to kill anything as to get away from our miserable little interior of dirt and smoke-grimed ceiling beams, cobwebby rafters, and windows through which the fowls came to pick up the unswept crumbs from the floor. Kitchen and dining-room in one was as dirty as sleeping and sitting-room, even though Pete had so far revolutionised appearances as to make H —— suspect him of wasting time in the very necessary job of cleaning up. So it was a relief to go up the mountains after deer, even if I mostly killed none. It was a good place for hunting, and a good time, for the snow on the upper hills drove them down, and I could, if I hunted carefully, often see them. I hardly ever shot at them, but stood watching. One day I saw either an elk or a most majestic deer, and would certainly have killed him if he had not been too quick for me. Then I could watch an occasional fox or the long-haired grey squirrels with their winter fur. And I usually got drenched through and through, and came back soaking to attend to the horses and the cattle, for nobody else would do it.

So time went, and my month began to draw to a close. My affectionate regard for my employer did not increase with more knowledge, as I found him selfish, close, and querulous, and, in spite of my previous experiences when out of employment, I determined to leave at the end of the month if he would not increase my wages to at least 15 dols. a month, and go across the Great Coast Range to Crescent City, and thence to San Francisco. So the night on which I had completed my term I spoke to him, and was refused any advance. He paid what was owing to me, 8 dols. 75 cents, for I had had some tobacco and one or two other things. Next day, however, it began to rain furiously without ceasing, and the creeks got full and overflowing, and a passing neighbour told us the Illinois River was not fordable. At noon H—— told me I could stay till it cleared up if I liked, on condition of working, and so for nearly a week I did all the stable work and odd jobs as usual. During this last seven days I walked over to Waldo to see if I could get some letters I thought would be lying there for me from Hughes, to whom I had written on my first arrival on this ranche. I had to cross the river on a big flume or aqueduct built to carry water across the river to a ditch for a hydraulic mine. The sight beneath me was magnificent. The river was fairly roaring in its rocky channel, red and turbid, running ten or twelve miles an hour, beaten into foam on the huge rocks in its midst and hurling the spray into the air, while the flume on which I stood trembled with the burden of water it carried and the shock of the stream below. I found letters at Waldo from my friend at Kamloops, and next day I left Mr. H—— and set out over the Coast Range.

CHAPTER XIX.

ACROSS THE COAST RANGE.

I HAD made preparations for a three or four days' walk, packing up some bread, bacon, and a little tea with a small bag of parched maize or Indian corn, while I put some stripped from the cob, but unparched, in my pockets. I had no exact knowledge of the distance to Crescent City in California, from which steamers ran to San Francisco, but knew it was between seventy and ninety miles or thereabouts, and, of course, as the road was very lonely, it was necessary to be provided with food. And then my finances would not have permitted me to pay for my meals, even if I had been able to buy them, inasmuch as the fare from Crescent to San Francisco was, I had been told, about 7 dols.

The week's rain and storm that had kept me from travelling had had a terrible effect on the roads. At stated intervals during the summer it was usual to run a stage from Waldo to Crescent, but this was now abandoned for the present for great part of the way, owing to the roads being 'washed out.' The rainfall had been terrific at the ranche, for at least an inch and a half fell in ten hours one night, and the wind had done some damage. There were vague reports of disasters on the coast, which most probably arose more from the likelihood of such occurring than from actual knowledge. What was of more importance to me were the facts that the Illinois was still unfordable, necessitating a *détour* over the flume, and that all the creeks in the valley were likely to be very full; and I found, after passing Waldo, that I had occasionally some difficulty in crossing one or two, while the road itself was muddy and full of pools of water. I walked, however, in good spirits until nightfall, and camped about twelve miles beyond Waldo, at the foot of the range, in a miserable hut with no doors or windows or flooring. All possible wood had been burnt by other travellers, and I had great difficulty in kindling a fire, partly from the scantiness of fuel and partly from the dampness of everything. I took my knife and scraped off the outer bark of a big fir-tree close at hand, and took some of the dry under bark; then I gathered up little bits of sticks, putting them inside my shirt to dry; finally, I took some gum or pitch from an old axe-cut in the tree, and with the aid of a letter from a friend in London, who little thought to what end his letter would come, or in what way aid me, I managed to make a poor blaze and to keep it in long enough to boil some water for tea. I need not have taken so much trouble if I had cared about tearing some of the shingles from the little hut, but I never liked to do that. There are some men who will always do this, but I had some little consideration for those coming after me, and if every one camping in a place took some of the building for a fire there would soon be no shelter.

I cooked a little bacon, ate that and a piece of bread, and drank the cup—the tin cup—of tea. Then I went into the shanty and spread my blankets. There was every prospect of a bitterly cold night, for it was now getting towards the end of November. The wind was chilly, and moaned outside and came through the openings and cracks of my abode. My blankets were old and thin, and the ground even inside was damp. My fire outside was now extinguished, with but a smouldering ember the wind puffed into momentary redness and a little wreath of smoke, and there was no wood to make one inside without aid of an axe. The situation was lonely and dismal. Below me ran the creek, not singing sweetly and placidly, but groaning and hurrying. Thick forest went back to the hills all round, while overhead the sky, moonless and chill, showed frequent clouds and an infrequent fugitive star. The nearest house was three miles from me, down the road on which I had come, and was uninhabited. To make matters worse I got an attack of nervousness, a thing most unusual with me, so that my imagination became heated, creating panthers, cougars, and bears, that would come and devour me in the night. To be sure there were these animals somewhere on the hills, but hitherto they had never alarmed me, not even in the Selkirks, where they were really numerous, and here they were scarce. I tried to lull myself with the notion that it was late enough in the season for the bears to be in their winter quarters, fast asleep and dreaming, but all the time I knew I was but deceiving myself, and every howl of wind I converted into a growl of nocturnal predacious animal—bear or wolf or mountain lion. And it grew colder and colder, until it was nearly freezing. I lay on my right side and dropped off into uneasy slumber. Presently I woke and found my left side nearly frozen, so I turned over and lay awake for awhile until that side grew a little warmer. Again I went to sleep, and woke once more with a start to find the other side cold. So went the night, until at last I woke, shivering all over, in the very earliest dawn, finding a white frost outside. I made a little fire again, drank some tea, and started off before it was fairly light, recovering courage and confidence as I grew warm with walking hard and climbing. The road was fairly good, and I had no dangerous creeks to cross. I climbed up and up in the fresh morning air, with bright sunlight above me and no fear or threatening of rain, until I was far above the valleys in a very winding road. The hills were not covered in all places by timber, and I could see far across the depths, which were filled with glistening clouds or mists, beneath me.

About seven o'clock I came round a turn in the road that ran high up the hillside above a deep valley or gorge, that was filled with cloud. The sun was behind me, and here, to my great delight, I saw a similar phenomenon to the Spectre of the Brocken. On the dense white fleece of cloud was a sun ring or halo, and in it, magnified to gigantic size, my own figure. I threw down my blankets and shouted with joy. I was all alone with my own ghost, my enlarged and liberated cloud-spirit, my likeness, but great, spiritual, free, apotheosised, among the gods. And from cloudland he returned my salute as I took off my hat, and waved his arms as I waved mine. I was free there from grossness; I was etherealised, idealised, poetic. And what a background even for a spirit, for a god! The little valley of my sun-shadow ran out into a larger one, filled with a sea of glistening cloud that lay still in places, or rolled and heaved solemnly like a light sea freed from the heavy chains of gravity. It lay not level, but in hills and long upward curves, indicating faintly the possible outline of the under hills, and here and there one loftier height thrust through the veiling mist fir and pine, like a far ocean palm island, when the island is not seen, and the trees are unbased and dreamlike, fantastic, divided from earth, and skyey. And the mass of mist was white, shining, fleecy and glorious, while beyond miles of it rose higher range after range, with the farthest capped with frost and snow, glittering like diadems of jewels.

I looked long and breathed in that air, and turning I bowed solemnly to my cloudself, who bowed again. I took up my burden and walked on in a curious state of mental exaltation, oblivious of the future and the past, regarding simply the scenery, the sun and the clouds beneath and above me. Yet the walk was arduous enough, though the worst was to come, for I was climbing up and going down all the while, while the road took most disappointing turns, and frequently I could have saved miles of tramping had I had wings to fly across a narrow valley or gorge round the head of which the road ran. Still I felt so well, for my nervousness had fled with the night, that I did not grumble, and when I came at noon to a good cabin, or house, I made dinner with care and sang while I prepared my frugal meal. This house belonged to a man named Bain, who had a notice put up on the door asking travellers to be careful of fire, and I thanked him for the hospitality of open door by writing a few lines of rude verse on the name-scrawled wall with a burnt stick, signing myself 'A Tramp.' I had no notion of any place to camp in at night, though I thought it possible that I might reach Smith River, on which there was an hotel, as I had been told by Angus H——. So I walked on cheerfully enough, meeting not a soul on the road, and at last it began to grow towards evening without any sign of a house or river. About half an hour before sundown I was walking along the road on the side of the hill, and across the valley, which was deep and thick with trees, I could see that I should have to make my way in exactly the opposite direction to which I was then going, after coming to the head of the gorge. This, of course, rather irritated me, although my anger was unreasonable, as the road was just so long, and I could not make it shorter. Still such a round made me anxious to camp, as the road, I could see, made quite a fresh start up the hill, and evidently Smith River must be many miles away yet.

Finally, I plunged deep in the valley, and I found at last a kind of broken-down hut or house, with a roof on, by the side of a creek, in silence and shadow. I looked at it for awhile and sat down, but the aspect of the place was so forbidding, so chill and damp, and so fearfully lonely, that I took up my blankets again and walked on, chewing corn as I went, determined not to stop or stay until I came to the river and the hotel. I came out just at sundown on the top of a very high ridge, and I fancied I caught a faint glimpse of far sea, but was not sure. It rapidly grew dark, and I walked hard and harder. Finally, there appeared a deep valley, or cañon, in front of me, with a narrow streak of silver turbulent river 4,000 feet below, and opposite another wall of mountain westward. I plunged down the road, and I fancied I saw the gleam of a far-off light close by the river. The descent was difficult and dangerous. The rains had washed out the earth and gravel and smaller stones of the surface of the road, so that it was like going down the dried bed of a mountain torrent. Every hundred yards or so the way zigzagged to and fro, seeking the easiest way down. Twice I fell, and times innumerable I only just saved myself. At last it grew so dark that I could only distinguish the road by the absence of brush. And the roar of the river below grew louder and louder. After an hour and a half's hard stumbling over rocks I came on to level ground, alongside the river, and with difficulty at last found a bridge across, and saw the lights of a house near at hand. This was my resting-place for the night.

Inside the main room were two men, one with a wooden leg, the owner of the establishment, a great hunter in spite of his infirmity, and the driver of the stage from Waldo, who had passed me during the night as I slept and shivered in that hut. There were two women, wife and sister-in-law of the one-legged man, a child, and two hunting-dogs. There was a good wood fire, and I was glad to sit down and smoke in front of it, being little inclined for talking. Soon after I came in supper was announced, but I declined taking any, my ostensible reason being that I had had supper before coming down into the valley, and the real one that I was anxious to keep all the money I could in my pocket for my San Franciscan fare. I was hungry enough, however, and could well have enjoyed a good meal. However, I promised myself a breakfast. That night I slept on a lounge or sofa in my own blankets, and was charged nothing for accommodation, so I only spent 50 cents for my morning meal. After eating I started to go up the opposite mountain, which took me about two hours' hard climbing up another zigzag of a road. On the top was a kind of plateau, almost bare of trees, and it was easy walking, with a fine view of mountains behind me. At noon I went down into another valley, coming on a deserted mining town of several houses and two hotels, with all the furniture removed, including doors and window-sashes. This desolation of past habitation made the scene more chill and lonely than if there had been no dwellings at all. I was very hungry, so I lighted a fire and boiled some tea.

In the bar-room of the largest hotel I found the hindquarters of a deer that had been left by some hunter, possibly by my one-legged acquaintance, and although it was somewhat flyblown I found it fresh, and by aid of my bowie-knife I managed to get some good pieces of steak, which I toasted on a sharpened stick over the fire. Then I cooked some bacon.

I had now a choice of roads—one the old and the other the new. The former was the shortest, the latter the best. After some consideration I chose the old road, and had some frightful scrambling over rocks, at times, too, having difficulty in discovering what was the road and what was not. Finally, I got in better walking on a gentle slope. I was now eagerly looking for sight of the ocean. The Gulf of Georgia and the Straits of San Juan de Fuca, the land-locked waters of Puget Sound, were but salt water; they lacked the enchantment of the sea. And I came over the long ridge, and before me was the deep sea—not a gulf or a channel or a strait, but the mighty main, the vast and tremendous waters of the mysterious Pacific, misty and grand, the ocean that Balboa saw from the silent peak in Darien. I sat down quietly on a knoll of dwarf manzanita, so still and quiet that the shy birds came and sang to me, and a wondering rabbit peeped from the brush and played before me; and as I drank in that sweet fresh air and watched the majestic expanse of far faint blue I seemed to see that the earth was round, huge, and curved; and beyond the horizon I saw, with spiritual insight and in trance, the long brown plains of the great Australian continent, whereon I too had wandered in the years passed by; and in front lay the long coasts of ancient populous Asia; and yet farther beyond that illimitable expanse, far across zones of calm and cyclones of wind storm, and belts of terrible thunder-cloud, lay the shores of the Dark Continent, full of mystery. And Europe, my home and birthplace, was behind and beneath me.

I thought of Vasco Nuñez, the discoverer of this ocean; of Magellan, who had blundered through the narrow straits that bear his name, and of Vasco di

Gama, who had entered on its waters round the far-off stormy Cape; of Pizarro, on those shores of Peru to the southward; and of our Drake, who chased the Spaniards through these seas; and I drew in with ecstasy the air that all those strong old voyagers and sea-captains had breathed in the times when something was yet unknown, and there were possibilities of Eldorados unmarked on any chart, when charts were graved on horns with strange adornment of gaping, imaginary sea-monsters, such as the young Amyas Leigh wondered at in the etched ivory of Salvation Yeo.

And I looked still, and the mystic water grew alive, subtle, serpentine, and more mysterious, coiling and wonderful. She became eyed like the peacock's tail, with faint eddies of currents, and personal and feminine. This was the ocean from which the earth arose, this was the grave to which she descended to be renewed; and the eyes grew intense and vivid, prophetic and full of kindness unutterable, and of cruelty. In her was the beginning of all things and the end; she and the sky were time and space, and symbolic. From her came the primæval slime of life, and she was full of dead men's bones. Ships sailed on her bosom, and in her depths they lay shattered, broken, sunken, dwelling-places for her monsters, evil as the thoughts that never pass men's lips. Her eyes were as those of one who knew all things, and her lips were touched with the melancholy of cruelty satiated, and yet her hands and fingers were eager for slaughter. She was calm and silent as a handmaiden of Fate, but passionate in her hair and eyes even as a sleeping fury; for in her dwell all things evil and good, and all knowledge and all power and all possibility of being.

And there was more of grief than of joy in my heart, for I remembered I was a man, and finite, and the spirit of my race, and the desire of love came upon me, and while the birds sang, and fearless squirrel and rabbit played in the wind-rustled manzanita and the slender grasses, I was oppressed and cold at heart, and I was glad to take up my burden and the burden of life and walk on and on, to save myself from thought. So I walked on downward, for I had done with climbing, and I saw in the far distance, across the level lands between sea and mountain base, the smoke of Crescent City. Down narrow paths, and all winding ways, through roads cut deep with the wash of rains, I still went on, among brush and a few scanty trees. And at last I plunged into a dark forest and a steeper path, and as I stumbled over bare roots and rocks I grew wrathful, and cursed the whole Pacific from Behring's Straits to the southern unknown lands of the South Pole, from San Francisco to African Zanzibar, and the Pacific coast and Horace Greeley, and the strange longing that had brought me West. For it grew darker yet, and still no sign of habitation or indication of nearing any, while

I came down into mist and fog, damp, chill and penetrating, making the gloom worse, hanging in wreaths among the thick growth of trees, touching brush with damp dews that dropped on me as I walked. Twice and again I fell and rolled over, the last time wrenching my ankle severely; but I walked in spite of it, desperately determined not to camp out in a gloomy place if perseverance could bring me to a better. And suddenly the path grew level, and I came out in the aisle of a very forest cathedral. I was in the redwoods, the most majestic of all trees, save only their elder brethren, the gigantic sequoias. These were huge and solemn, some ten feet and more in diameter at the butt, rising bare of branches to 200 feet above me, where they spread out in thick crowns, that darkened yet more the obscure and misty air of night. I stood for a few moments to admire them, even tired as I was, and then with difficulty I discovered the road. I found that it forked here. I stood and considered again. The straight road was most probably the road to the town, the other would probably lead to some house or camp. I determined to turn off, and as a reward for my reasoning I saw a light less than a hundred yards away. I passed through the barn-yard and knocked and went in. There were two men, rather well dressed, and a very ladylike woman. We talked for a while and they gave me supper, and said I could sleep in the barn. The hay was wringing wet, through the leaks in the roof, but I managed to get to sleep in spite of any inconveniences after the walk I had had, and next morning I had still thirteen miles to do to reach Crescent City, and I started without breakfast, and did the whole distance wearily and fasting. My road ran still through the redwoods, and if they were solemn and weird at night they were more beautiful in the daytime. Under them at times was thick brush, from which they rose like towers or great lighthouses from the breaking of little waves, and in other places they stood by themselves, springing straight from the bare ground, or moss, or scanty turf. These had grown for so many centuries, and had such great life in them, they were so grand and solemn and kinglike, that I felt they had personality. It seemed nothing short of murder to hew and saw them down for planks and post-making, for house-building, and shelter for little men, who lusted to destroy in an hour the slow, sweet growth of their unnumbered years. We come with our quick and furious flood of life to a quick conclusion ; they, with the slow sap under bark and in the wood, rise imperceptibly to majesty, and fall at the end of their long term by overgrowth of summit and crown ; they sink at last under the burden of natural honours, and mingle slowly in long decay with the soil in which they were rooted. But men come and destroy them, as barbarians in the pathetic, silent senate-house, and nature is wounded and bleeding.

T

I came out on the banks of the Smith River again and was ferried over, and was asked no fee. I was astonished at the lack of greed, and the natural sweet kindliness of the man, a Charon fair and young, which is so rare in all countries, and, alas! much too rare in America. I thanked him courteously, and he bowed and wished me well most knightlike, pushing back across the stream, and I passed again into the redwoods, climbing up through a sweet tangle of thick brush with the great god-trees rising from it, and then descended and came on a flat, more bare, with willow and birch, and no more redwoods. And I began to hear a faint roar, like a singing in my ears. But it grew and grew till I recognised the sound of the sea, the roar of breakers, the eternal ocean voice. It put new life into me; I walked faster, though I was faint, until I came where I could hear the separate roar of separate waves—distinct thunders. I sat down under a tree by the roadside and lighted my pipe, and, to save myself from vain imaginings of possible things, I took my Virgil and again read part of the Sixth Book. And when I came to the middle I thought, 'I am not yet out of Avernus, and who knows if I shall return to the lucid stars and lucid earth, for there is much to be passed through before my time is at hand.'

So I came at last to Crescent City, and found it dull and vile, with work scarce, so they said, and men plenty. I was truly in golden California, but not in the land of wine and oil, of fleeces and fat beeves. Being hungry and disconsolate, it was necessary to eat, and I ate the worth of 25 cents and was more refreshed. The steamer for San Francisco was lying in the bay, loading timber, and was to sail in the night, having been delayed by the storm, which had torn away part of the pier and driven driftwood upon the very streets of the town. So I went to buy my ticket. Now Angus H—— had told me the fare was 7.50 dols. As I had started on this last journey with 8.50 dols., and had only spent three-quarters of a dollar—50 cents at the Smith River Valley and 25 cents in town—I had 7.75 dols., which would leave me 25 cents with which to make a start in San Francisco. But when I got to the office they demanded 8.50 dols. as the fare, and I had it not. I used much persuasive eloquence and rhetoric to induce the agent to make a reduction, opening up fully the state of my finances. But he was adamantine, flinty, and I could make no impression on him. I appealed to the chief man, a general of militia, and calling him General I asked him to 'fix' it for me. But no! he would do nothing. The fare, the full fare, and nothing but the fare. So I went out to consider. To walk to San Francisco meant 300 miles of semi-starvation at least if I did not obtain work. I furiously determined to go by that steamer or perish in the attempt. I took stock of my possessions. Had I anything to sell? My clothes might have been worthy of acquisition by a museum of antiquities, but even then I could not go in that vessel 'Berserker.' My blankets were old and thin; besides, I attached a superstitious value to them. They were part of myself. Had they not travelled in Australia with me over hill and plain? Had they not been wet with salt water in my voyages? And they had done me great service in great need in all parts of America. No! I would as soon part with my skin. Then I had a bundle of letters from men who might be celebrated one day, literary Bohemians of London, who had not forgotten their Waring on his travels. There were photographs too. But these would not fetch money in the market. Finally, I came to my Horace and Virgil. Was it possible there were men with a knowledge of the Latin tongue in this wilderness, this end of the earth? Or were there some burning with thirst to acquire such knowledge? I walked up the street and came to a notice:—

WALTER JONES, B.A., Advocate,
Teacher of Latin, Greek, and Mathematics.

Ye gods! I stared, thinking I was dreaming! This was the man. I pushed open the door and entered, acting on the spur of the moment. I saw a little sad-looking man, with a good forehead and shabby clothes. There were lots of books there too. He received me courteously and asked my business. I sat in silence for a moment, wondering if he thought I wished to learn Latin or Greek or even mathematics. Then I told him I wanted to get to San Francisco, and then, interrupting me nervously, he said:

'If it's money you want, I'm very sorry, but I haven't got any myself.'

'I'm not surprised,' I answered, 'that an educated man should be without in such a brutish wilderness. But I did want money—75 cents—and I want to sell you this Horace or Virgil for it.'

'I can't, I can't, I haven't got a cent, and I'm in debt too. But perhaps you could sell it to Father Grady, the Roman Catholic priest.'

'Is he an Irishman?'

'Yes.'

'Then I don't want anything to do with him. I have a premonition of the kind of man, and somehow I don't like Irishmen, especially if they are religious.'

'Well, I can't do anything for you but that. I m really sorry. I could see, when you spoke, that you were an educated man, and I would do anything I could for you. But I am positively unable to make a living here myself.'

I was sorry for him. He looked ill and weak. I was at any rate well and strong, and could do manual labour.

'Well, thank you, Mr. Jones. I suppose I must try the reverend father.'

'Yes, do, and come and tell me how you get on with him.'

I shook hands with the little man and made my way to the priest's house. He came out to me. I was right. He was just the kind of low-class peasant Irishman that I detest most cordially. The very look of him made me half sick, and I very nearly turned away without speaking. However, I opened my business to him, and told him Mr. Jones had sent me. 'Thank you, I don't want either of them. I know them by heart already' (said I to myself, 'You lie'), 'and I have copies with me of course. But you might try Mr. So-and-so' (I forget the name) 'the hotel-keeper.'

I thanked him as civilly as I could, which was not over courteously, for my gorge so rose against his fat conceit and complacency.

I found the hotel-keeper. He was an intelligent man, but half-drunk. 'Yes, I am something of a classical scholar, but I don't read these books now. I don't want 'em.' Then a look came into his eyes I could not quite fathom. 'But,' said he, 'do you see that tall man down the road, with a plank on his shoulder?' 'Yes,' said I. 'Then you go and ask him. He's the best scholar in this city, bar old Jones.'

I turned away and went after the man with the plank. I had serious doubts, when I came close to him, as to his scholarship. Good-natured idiocy seemed more his intellectual station among men than learning.

I went up and told him that the hotel-keeper had sent me. He burst into a roar of laughter. 'Ho! ho! ho! Why, man, I can't read or write at all. Ho! ho! ho!' and he put his plank down and sat on it to laugh at his case. I was in a fearful rage. I turned to go back and assault my jocose friend, but as I went along I thought, 'If I do they'll have me in gaol too quick, and I have no friends here at all.' So I thought better of it and restrained myself, although I was fairly boiling. It would have gone hard with him, even after second thoughts, if I had met him face to face.

I went back to the office and tackled the General once more, but in vain. Then I determined to jump on the steamer in spite of them, and if I got on and out to sea they should have no fare at all. If I could not manage to get on board with the other passengers when they went off to her I would borrow a boat and try to get on her in the dark. So I went down in the evening and found a crowd of people waiting until the boat was ready for them. A big barge, or scow, laden with lumber was to take them. When word was given for the passengers to come forward I tried to get down, but the agent or clerk was too smart for me, and demanded my ticket. I had none, of course. Then the fare. 'How much?' said I, as if I didn't know.

'Eight and a half dollars.'

'I've only got seven dollars and six bits.'

'Then stand back.'

So down the others went until I was left alone on the pier with the clerk and one or two lookers-on. He came over to me.

'How much did you say you had?'

I told him.

'All right, you can go. Hand over.'

I handed over, and then said: 'You may as well leave me two bits to get a meal with in San Francisco.'

He looked and hesitated a moment, then gave me back the twenty-five cents. I thanked him and went down to the scow, and presently we got on board. I had 'made that riffle' at any rate, and was not compelled to risk the 'conveying' of boats and stowing away.

When we got on board I went down into the steerage and found one more white man and four Chinamen in it. This place was a veritable Black Hole. There were four double bunks, each holding two men, a big chest in the small space between the bunks, and the rest of it was taken up by the steps. The only light came from the hatch above, and was supplemented by an evil-smelling oil lamp. I am cosmopolitan enough, Heaven knows, and have consorted with all sorts and conditions of men—Australian blacks, Hindoos, Malays, Japanese, Indians, and all kinds of Europeans —but of all I have been thrown into contact with I most thoroughly detest the low Chinese. And now

I had to spend two whole days, at least, in close quarters with them. I chummed in with the white man, who was a nice, good-looking young fellow—a milker and butter-maker—and slept in the same bunk with him; but we had to eat with the Chinese, and as they were violently sick when we got out to sea they managed to make things very unpleasant. I stayed on deck as much as possible, and when I did go below I went there to sleep. Yet these two days are black ones in my calendar, though blacker ones were yet to come to me. On the evening of the second day we came to the Golden Gate, and ran through it into the great bay of San Francisco. It was a beautiful sight, but I was too melancholy and anxious to enjoy the sight of sea and cliff, of lighthouse and quiet shining water, and the hills gleaming in the setting sun that sank behind us. As we passed up the harbour the city was gradually lighted up with gas and electricity, and the waters grew gloomy and gloomier yet. We threaded our way through ships at anchor, and passed dark wharves with others loading or discharging, and at last made fast ourselves to the wharf at the foot of Mission Street. Outside on the wharf were numerous 'buses to hotels, and as we touched the sides we were boarded by a crowd of hotel-runners, shouting and screaming: 'The International,' 'The American Exchange,' 'The Russ House,' and eulogising the merits of a dozen others. The man from the 'American Exchange' came to me as I sat on my blankets smoking, and was most urgent I should go with him, and would not let me alone. At last I turned to him, and said: 'It's no good, partner, I'm no catch. I'm dead broke.' He left me, and when things began to get a little quieter I picked up my bundle and went over the side. I was again in a strange city, and all that I had was 25 cents—one shilling, and a halfpenny over.

CHAPTER XX.

IN SAN FRANCISCO.

IN the steamer I had had plenty of opportunity for reflection as to the course to be pursued on arrival in San Francisco, but all the mental exercise had resulted in was the conclusion that I should be in a very bad fix indeed when I got there, and that I should, if possible, leave it at once. As it was a great shipping port, in fact *the* port of the whole Pacific coast, my mind naturally turned to going to sea again if nothing else turned up. So when I slung my blankets on my back and walked along the city front towards the better-lighted portions of the city, I determined to look for a sailors' boarding-house, the proprietor of which would take me in if sailors were at all in demand. I came in front of what I afterwards found out was called the Ferries, at the foot of Market Street, and went to where there were a lot of saloons, eating-houses, boot-black stands, peanut vendors, and newspaper sellers, and asked a man to direct me to a sailors' boarding-house. He pointed to the saloon before me and I went in, and asking for the boss told him I was a sailorman, and that I wanted to find a house, acting in a jaunty, devil-may-care manner.

'Hev you got any money?' 'Nary cent.' 'Then I can't do anything for you. Hell ain't fuller of devils than San Francisco is of sailors, and most of them dead broke. My house is full up now. Perhaps you might stand a show at the Arizona Hotel on Clay.' He came outside and showed me which way to go. In Clay Street, a dirty dark narrow way, I found the other house, and had no better luck there. I asked the proprietor to let me leave my blankets for a while. Then I went out and found another house, and was again refused, this time roughly, and without courtesy such as the other two to whom I had applied had extended to me. It must be remembered that I looked rough enough to be a sailor a dozen times over, and I could very well affect the old sailor roll, which now was no longer natural to me. So I looked like one who had been taking a spell in the country. However, it was no good trying these houses, and after talking for a while with a sailor, who confirmed the statements of the boarding-house keepers about the numbers of idle men in the city, I thought I would go and look for a lodging. I found one in Clay Street, and after paying 20 cents for my bed I put my blankets in the trunk-room and went in and sat down in the sitting-room. There were more than twenty men in this place, which was bare of adornment save a quack doctor's advertisement on the walls. The tables were wood uncovered and somewhat hacked with knives, the floors were dirty and covered with saliva, old chews, and tobacco ash, while two or three spittoons of rubber were full to overflowing. There were chairs, however, and not benches, as in many lodging-houses. The denizens of the place were not to me, after what I had seen, in any way strange, but I fancy if some cultured, educated man direct from London civilisation had been dropped into the room he would have been struck by the scene. The room was well lighted with kerosine lamps, but a dense cloud of tobacco-smoke hung from the ceiling to the heads of those who were seated, and the gabble of tongues made the place a very Babel, for some were talking at the tops of their voices, some playing cards at the tables, laughing and occasionally even yelling, and there was a ring of others round the stove keeping up a loud and animated conversation with all the interest of a round game, in which victory remained with the longest and loudest talker, and ignominious defeat and forfeit to him who ceased first. Then there were others round the wall, some asleep in spite of the din, others with their chairs tilted back, sunk in coma or reflective study, and some with their heels on the vacant table, chewing tobacco and spitting with vast differences in accuracy of aim at the overburdened spittoons, one of which was most gruesome to see, and betraying occasionally faint gleams of aroused interest when a lucky shot was made in this modern American game of κότταβος.

The faces, figures, and dresses of these men were as various as their moods, attitudes, and occupation, and after a little while spent in quiet observation, with my chair tilted back against the wall, the differences began to be very perceptible to me. One of the loudest talkers was an American Irishman, and his professional occupation was evidently something to do with coal, as I noticed the grime of coal-dust round his eyes, which comes off only after repeated washings. He was slight, dressed in blue dungaree trousers and an old shiny black coat. His face was merry and red, and his brown eyes twinkled as he made a joke at a stolid-looking Swede or German, with a face as motionless as a block of wood, who, nevertheless, at times let out a flood of broken English which I could scarcely understand. There was another, manifestly a sailor, rather smartly dressed, with a bright face and a red knotted handkerchief under it. He was evidently at home, and noisier than a man of forty usually is when sober. There was a big, heavy German, whom they addressed as 'Bismarck,' who sat playing casino, or seven up, or some other card game, sometimes joining vigorously in the talk and thumping the table till the lamp jumped and the light flickered up the chimney. Then there was a very fine, handsome-looking young fellow, who was a cigar-maker as I found out afterwards, with well-cut features and a pleasant laugh, who usually sat with his heels on the table.

There were men, too, who looked as if they did

nothing—'bums' in fact—others whose trade it was a puzzle to discover, and some who seemed, like myself, to be from the country. It was a curious mixed gang, and I was glad at last to take my lamp and go to bed in a little narrow room, in which the bed took up most of the space. There were nearly two hundred of these apartments, separated from each other by wooden partitions with an open roof covered with a mosquito netting, and I could hear the snoring of my neighbours in various keys, and notes from deep bass to shrill treble, while one or two ran through the whole gamut, some occasionally choking and waking themselves.

In the morning it was a very serious question with me. I had five cents—$2\frac{1}{2}d.$—and no prospect of breakfast. Of course I was hungry, and the fact that it seemed impossible to appease the growing famine made me worse. I walked out and up and down to consider things, and finally, after taking a smoke, I determined to go to the British Consul, to see if he could get me a ship. I found my way to his rooms near the Post Office, and had an interview, not with the Consul himself, who is an august and unapproachable person, but with a short stout man of sailor-like appearance, who heard my story, briefly told, and gave me a note to the captain of an English ship, asking him to ship me if possible. I went down, found the vessel, and after waiting dismally for two hours, kicking my heels on the wharf, and disconsolately watching the boats in the bay, I was told that the ship would not sail for six weeks and wanted no hands at present, as she had more than enough staying by her. Then I tried a dozen other vessels without success, and got so weary, hungry, and disgusted that I went back to Clay Street, and sat down in the house for an hour or two, still having a little tobacco to prevent me from suffering too acutely from famine. Then I went again to the Consul's, but got no encouragement there.

I went up Market Street and tried to divert my attention from myself by taking a look at the city, whose fine broad streets, and street cars or trams that run without horses, being drawn on an underground cable, had great attraction for me. I noticed, too, the cosmopolitan character of the place, the numerous races to be seen, and the beauty of many of the women; but as evening drew on the calls of hunger became so piercing that I went back again to my lodging-house, and sat down thinking where I should get something to eat and how to get a lodging. At last I determined to spend my last five cents, and going to a restaurant got a cup of coffee, telling the man that the 'nickel,' or five-cent piece, was my last money. He gave me a dough-nut to eat with the coffee. This was the first I had eaten for twenty-four hours. I thanked him and went back again to the house, thinking that I should have to spend the night in the streets. I sat down and got into conversation with the man next to me, and I opened up the talk by speaking about the state of things in the city, and he told me that thousands were out of work, and that there was every prospect of its being a hard winter to working men. Then I told him I was dead broke, and asked his advice as to where I should sleep. 'Well,' said he, 'the clerk here is a good fellow, and won't turn you out; you can stay in this room all night and sleep on a chair or on the floor. There's lots of fellows do it.' This was some consolation, for I did not desire to tramp about the city and spend the damp cold night in the open air. I asked the clerk at ten o'clock if he would let me stay, and he said that that would be all right if I came up when the others had gone to bed. At half-past eleven I came up, and he let me in the room, from which the lamps had been removed, and I found there five or six other men whom I had seen about the place during the evening. One was quite an old, respectable-looking man, another was a jolly-looking individual, who carefully spread some newspapers on the floor in the warmest corner and lay down on them. The others were nondescript fellows, rough and dirty. I drew a chair up to the stove and slept for an hour very uncomfortably, then I lay down on the bare boards and slept uneasily until four o'clock, when Jim, the clerk, came in and roused us up by calling out 'Breakfast,' which seemed to me a very poor joke indeed, as I was about as hungry as I could be. We went out and washed in the lavatory, looking a miserable lot of wretches, and I went down into the street, lighted dimly by lamps, for there was yet no sign of day.

It was absolutely necessary for me to get something to eat. It could be put off no longer. So, after thinking awhile, I went down to the wharf where the steamer in which I had come from Crescent City was lying, and had a talk with the night watchman, whom I asked to give me some breakfast. He gave me some coffee and bread and meat, which I ate ravenously, and went away thanking him for his kindness. I ate nothing else all day, and spent the time hunting for a ship, and at night slept on the bare boards as before. Next day I went in the forenoon to an employment office, not with any hope of getting employment, having no money for fees, but just to do something. But my luck was great. I sat down on a bench, above which was a notice board with requisitions for milkers, butter-makers, coachmen, choppers, and labourers of all sorts, among a crowd of men, some of whom I knew by sight, when in came my old friend of the Rockies and Eagle Pass Landing, Scott! I jumped up and we shook hands warmly. He was dressed well, and had a gold chain across his waistcoat. I was as rough-looking as possible, and just as I had been when I saw him last, save that my hat was new. He asked me how I was 'making it,' or getting along, and I told him just how it was with me. He gave me 25 cents, and I went out and got a 10-cent dinner at a cheap eating-house, where they give a great deal for the money. Scott had left Eagle Pass soon after me and had gone direct to Victoria, and then to San Francisco, where he had been for some weeks, working part of the time. The remaining 15 cents kept me for that day and the next, as I spent nothing for lodging, and then he gave me a little more. At the end of a week from the time I had come to the city he told me he had heard of a chance for work for me, and I went up to a store in Market Street, owned by a man whose possessions ran into millions of dollars. He told me to come round in the morning and I could get a day's work. I came accordingly at seven o'clock and went to work without having had breakfast, my supper the night before having consisted of a cup of coffee and a roll.

I helped two men, one a Swede, the other an Englishman, to clean out the cellar or basement of some new buildings, carrying up heavy timbers, iron boilers, bricks, and glass frames, hard work at any time, but laborious in the extreme on an empty stomach. However, my Englishman was a good little fellow, and lent me 15 cents, with which I got the best meal I had had in San Francisco. At night I got a dollar and a half, my day's wages, and was told to come again on Monday, as this was Saturday. I was now quite a capitalist, and by eschewing the luxury of a bed I could manage to live for some time. I worked again on Monday, and then my boss told me to come up to his private house next night, as he wanted a man to get some rock and gravel out of a quarry to fill up his yard and make a good floor. I was to sleep in the barn. I went up and lay in a loft among bales of hay and innumerable rats, who ran along the bales and then jumped on me, waking me up all night long. Sometimes half a dozen would charge across me at once, and if I made a noise it would only quiet them for a minute, and their games would begin again. In the morning I went to work in the quarry, and kept at it for ten days, taking all the dogs of the establishment to bed with me at night, whereby I saved myself from rats, but was troubled with fleas and an occasional fight over my recumbent figure.

My meals cost me a good deal during this time, so when I left I only had about nine dols., upon which I lived for nearly three weeks, still staying in Clay Street, where I now had a bed, paying a dollar a week for it.

Scott by this time was working in a Turkish bath-house, and was at any rate making a living.

I tried hard to get employment myself but without avail, and gradually my small store of silver got less and less as I went back into my old condition, even though I nearly starved myself, exercising great self-control in the matter of meals. And in these days I passed into the company of books, and in them found the only true nepenthe. They were a refuge and a consolation, for in them I sought strength for my weakness, and renewed courage, and did not seek in vain. They are indeed steadfast friends to the afflicted, and wise counsellors to the wavering and infirm, and but for them who can say what might have been my lot? If there are no fields of amaranth beyond the grave, there is even asphodel on this hither side, and in the company of the mighty men of old we wander at last in a discoverable Eden, and by the very borders of the fabled lakes of Elysium. For the end of culture is a salvation of the soul from all things foul and horrible, and the ghastly phantoms born of despair, whether it be engendered of the pestilential miasma of our lower humanity or the friendless desolation of utter misery.

I came down at last to no money at all, and in desperation I sent home for the 100 dols. which I had remitted to England in Kamloops. Then I had at least forty days to get through. Times were now terribly hard in San Francisco. It was estimated that there were at least 20,000 men out of work, to say nothing of women and children. Londoners have nowadays some faint notion of the struggle for life among the poor of London, and the unutterable miseries they suffer during a bad winter, but they still think that America is a paradise, and that there can be no want there, especially in the Golden West. But they are much mistaken.

I had to take again to sleeping on bare boards, and I was much luckier than many others, who slept in doorways, and on the piles of potatoes on the wharf, and sometimes went to the police station and got a bed there. Then there was a fearful struggle for food. I used to sit in the lodging-house room and hear men, whom I knew to be near starvation, telling each other of hotels and restaurants where they would give men food, warning each other not to go to others lest they should be given into custody. I knew one man who lived for months by going down to the iron-working places and machine shops in Mission Street, and asking the men who were lucky enough to have work to give him what was left when they finished their dinners. Another lived on a friend who used to bring twice as much as he could eat to work with him. Then some were without food for two days at a time. For my own part, Scott helped me considerably, and at last I found out a charitable organisation from whom I got much help, promising to repay them when I got my money from England, and I did so. The secretary was a fine, kind old fellow, and used to get me to clean the office windows, giving me a dollar for two or three hours' work, finding me a job at gardening sometimes.

He knew I was an educated man, and, in spite of

my appearance and poverty, treated me as an equal. Then at last I had quite a stroke of luck. I met in Clay Street, one day, John Anderssen, the Swede who had worked with me at the mill in New Westminster, and who had been with me on that terrible winter's walk. He took me down to a schooner and got me a job helping to discharge her. The work was fearfully heavy, and I had to run all day long dragging heavy planks; but the pay was good—four dols., or 16s. 8d., for nine hours. It is one of the hardest things a man can do, and there are thousands of working men who are unable to do it. Yet I stuck to it for a day and a half, when the work was done, and made six dols. This was quite a windfall, and I lived for two weeks on it, having a bed again, after three weeks on bare boards. It was now the beginning of 1886. But I hoped to get my money from England early in February, and then things would be better. Meantime I spent my time in walking round the city, with which I got thoroughly acquainted, and in reading in the library. Scott I saw at frequent intervals, and when I was in good spirits we used to renew our old discussions about religion, and he used to make me read the letters I wrote home, for he had a great admiration for my epistolary style, and considered me a complete letter-writer of a very high order.

Then at nights he used to take me off to some revival meeting, which would be more comic to me than any theatre, as the way such affairs were carried on was new to me, for I had never been to any before. I think Scott had a dim hope in his mind that I should be converted to active religion, but he was doomed to disappointment, as my sense of humour was too great for me to forget the rank absurdities of speech and demeanour of these apostles. It surprised me, however, to see with what fluency even manifestly uneducated people could tell their experiences, until at last I discovered that their method of talking, when they got stuck, was to interject a stream of 'Praise the Lords' until they thought of something else, finally attaining a rapidity of utterance in some cases worthy of the main demi-god of the platform, round whom would be sitting a circle of devout hysterical girls.

During these weeks of comparative ease, owing to my six dols., I never ceased trying to get work, but it was no use, and finally I got so disgusted that I left off trying, leaving things in the hands of Destiny. The number of men in town seemed, if anything, to increase, and the employment offices were fairly besieged by applicants. Some poor fellows actually committed suicide, and I saw more than one in the morgue who would have been alive, I doubted not, if work had been obtainable. I used sometimes to go to this morgue, not, I think, out of morbid curiosity, but simply from sheer *ennui*, when I felt incapable of reading. And it had generally an occupant or two, for San Francisco is fertile in violent deaths, and in five months I know there were ten murders at least. Murders I call them, though a corrupt bench and jury usually bring it in anything but that, and acquit the guilty person if he or she have sufficient money or influence.

In that same morgue I one night saw a woman lying dead—a woman with a most beautiful, calm face, splendid hair and delicate skin; a woman of a common history and the old perpetual tragedy of our life and society. Young and lovely, with a beautiful voice, she left her husband's home, God knows by what drawn or driven, and was for years an outcast in the streets of San Francisco, and yet, in spite of disease and want and drink, her fatal beauty remained with her scarcely diminished, and the touch of sudden death purified her and made her saintlike—to me at any rate, though I doubt if the group of ghouls around her thought so, though another wretched woman, her companion for years in the polluting and polluted ways of that vile city, sat by and wept bitterly with her face in her hands, and her hair dishevelled like the locks of an Eastern mourner.

For three months San Francisco was a city of sorrow and despair to me, of laborious occupation or worse, of none at all, of poverty, of starvation, of discomfort. When I think of those miserable nights on bare planks, in vile smell of tobacco, I shiver. It is a nightmare to think of myself standing outside in the dreary street, with my equally unlucky companions, looking up at the windows of the sitting-room, to which Jim would only allow us to come when the lights were removed, as sign that the rest had gone to bed. And the uneasy sleep and the dreams of better things, and the awakening to misery and starvation—it was bitter. The walk in Oregon, bad as it was, and the Selkirk trail are nothing, in my memory, to these most evil days in that city, when it seemed little indeed that kept me at times from the tables of the morgue. And even when brighter days came at last, and my long-expected money came from England, I could not help seeing the misery of others, which was so patent to me who had gone through it myself. In those days I was an Anarchist, a very Nihilist, and the sight of rich prosperity filled me with fury, and a millionaire was a loathsome object, a vampire, a bloodsucker. Even now I shiver to think of the horror of that time, when it seemed as if every avenue of hope was closed, and black necessity drove me slowly backward to the waters of suicide. It was at times vain to try to read; I only saw my own history in the pages, and the headings Misery and Starvation. It was vain to try to think of things past when I was bound to the wheel of the present, crushed and maimed. I had no patience, no hope, no charity. I was tortured by the lack of all human feelings in me. I was at times a brute and carnivorous. Then I grew sad and melancholy, no more savage and wild, and I sat down by myself in silence, and would have wept for sheer misery and utter loneliness had not my tears been dried up. And sometimes I grew almost delirious, and came into a new world, suffering from a calenture, viewing a mirage; and my veins bounded, and I was strong and wise, philosophic, calm and virtuous, and then cast down in utter confusion, sweeping like a lost boat over a cataract to the whirlpools of a lost soul. Yet at times I was merry, and laughed and joked with my fellows about our sufferings, and made light of them, and then went out cursing. And all this for lack of work, for lack of a little money, and because I had known other things, and was, it may be, cultured, and in many ways gifted beyond my poor brutish friends.

It was thus I learnt the misery of cities and the perpetual warfare and bitter fight for life. I have no need to go now to the slums of London in search of a new sensation. I will keep away unless I can do good there, for the sight of such misery would come back to me with more than a hundred times the effect it would have on even some delicate highborn lady, who from motives of compassion and curiosity has gone to the dreadful East-end in winter time. Do these not look at the sufferings they see as if the sufferers belonged to a lower, different race? It may not be so, but I fear it is too often. But I know I was even as these—starved, hopeless, miserable, passionate, hating, and their sight and memory are dreadful.

And how strange the contrast to me with a little money! New clothes, and a bath and plentiful meals.

Lo! a new man, careless, laughing, and too forgetful. The change was too sudden, and I changed too much, and for a time became callous. I had suffered; then let others suffer. I had starved; was I to help others, that I might perhaps the sooner starve again? Should I not take some luxury, because others lacked necessary things? I grew selfish and went off reading, or I took long walks to look at the sea breaking on the ocean beach, or the bright bay, to see things while I was in the humour for them. I thrust aside my past sufferings, and with them those of the rest. Yet this was but a reaction, I think. I had been strained almost to the breaking-point, and now I was let loose. I had been played up so harshly that more than one tuning was wanted to make me tolerable. I was weary of seeing evil when all things seemed evil. I was a passive Manichæan, on the whole on the side of good, but a non-combatant. Then between Good and Evil. There was no Good and Evil. It was 'thinking made it so.' Perhaps it was that

> 'A little discord makes My music sweet,'
> Saith God upon His throne; 'so let men beat
> Their painful breasts and moan.'

And my life ran in calmer channels as I sought vaguely for work, knowing that it would ere long be necessary, yet not striving earnestly for very lack of power. I passed into the world of books, remaining in the library for hours, and I read the 'Meditations of Marcus Antoninus' and Blake's 'Poems of Innocence' once and again, understanding much, and, I am fain to say, looking at some as a child might at Sanskrit in the Devanagari character—as something occult, mystic, hieroglyphic, and secret. In some other cities I should have spent much of my leisure in picture galleries—in Melbourne, for instance—but in this city of outer barbarians there is no such thing, and little art and few artists. Chromos and oleographs such as one sees in London are infinitely ahead of much water and oil painting in San Francisco; and to look at the many villanous daubs that hang there, even in good shops, was extremely painful to me, who at any rate had seen, and seen often, the best in London—Turner, Danby, Gainsborough and Reynolds, and Rossetti's marvellous morbid work, and all the old schools, Italian and Venetian, and Lionardo da Vinci, and had sat and dreamed vague dreams unexpressed anywhere or by anybody, except by Pater's words on La Gioconda, and who had read Ruskin over and over again. Then even etchings and engravings were from old worn-out European plates, and were ghastly. So I was forced back to Nature again, and yet went willingly, and sat for hours on a rock on the ocean beach and heard the sea thunder, and saw the white foam lightning on the dark blue of the turbulent waters, taking good care to turn my back to the cliffs that soulless, enterprising Americans had placarded with advertisements of champagnes and brandies unknown to European merchants, such as Piper-

Heidsieck. Or I went up Telegraph Hill, above the bay, and saw the huge ferry boats running to Oakland, Alameda, San Rafael or Saucelito with foam tracks behind them, and the merchant ships lying at anchor with delicate tracery of rope and spar against the calm water, or the opposing hills, above which rose the winter-crowned crest of Mount Diablo or Tamalpais, and heard the near current of humanity on the wharves and the roar of traffic and handling of far-brought merchandise.

At last it was undoubtedly time for me to be at work, for living even in dreamland costs money, and the veriest Buddha has to live on victuals and drink. In the middle of April I received an offer of work on a ranche in Lake County, to the north of San Francisco, on the condition that I should engage myself for a year. Having still some money left, I declined to put myself in such fetters and shackles, knowing that the very fact of its being impossible for me to leave would inevitably make me anxious to do it. But in the beginning of May I began to feel very anxious, for my hoarded dollars decreased one by one. I went to a great bookseller's in town and undertook the work of a 'book agent.' I had to wander round the city with a large sample atlas under my arm, going into every place I thought might offer me a chance to dispose of one, and suffered during some days the misery of trying to induce a man who manifestly was not in need of my book to nevertheless buy it.

The successful book agent is a man who can read character, who is pliable, ready, quick-witted, and not to be repulsed. He must have brains, but cheek, impudence, or what is often called 'gall' in America, is far more necessary, and it was most decidedly in this that I was lacking. I sold a few and made 40 per cent. on my sales, but 80 or 100 per cent. would not have compensated me for the shame and diffidence I experienced in entering house after house for a whole day, with perhaps only one success to be scored to me, and only too often I worked hard and made nothing at all. Finally, after three days, which were absolutely blank, I sold my sample copy at a sacrifice, and renounced a business for which I was evidently unfit.

In the second week of May my luck began to turn. I had come down at last to five dollars, then four, three, two, one, and then I had none at all. I was dead broke again, and without prospects. Up to this time I had dwelt in a fool's paradise, and was a kind of dreamy Micawber, but the rude shock of finding myself again without cash awoke me like a cold douche, and I set to work 'rustling' for a job. And as it was spring there was some likelihood of my being able to find it, even if I had to put my old blankets on my back once more and go out into the vast Californian country on speculation. But by a happy chance this was spared me, and I was glad, for it would have been most extremely bitter for me to have made another tramp like my British Columbia or Oregon journeys, perhaps in starvation and suffering once more. I had met a certain English merchant in San Francisco, a man of wealth and many ranches. To him I applied for employment. He could give me none, and sent me away disconsolate, but the day after I received a message from him, and the next morning found me on my way to Sonoma County, to work upon a vineyard and stock and grain ranche. The wages were but small—20 dols. a month—and I found the work sufficiently arduous, but I made up my mind to stay there in spite of everything until I had enough money to take me back to England, for after being out in the cold so long I desired to feel the warm air of civilisation on my cheeks once more.

The situation of the ranche was beautiful. At the back of the farm buildings rose a precipitous mountain clothed on its lower slopes with fir and birch and pine, while above the trees ran rocky peaks that shone rosy red in the summer's setting sun. Across the valley rose another chain of hills more bare of timber, and the lands between us and this farther range were green with vines and golden with wheat and corn and barley. From the higher peaks of the mountain I saw the waters of San Francisco's bay, and at times the haze and smoke of the city itself, while nearer lay mapped out beneath me farm after farm and vine plot after vine plot, verdant and flourishing.

My work was very various, and required a man who had some knowledge of many things, and certainly I think my experience had so far fitted me for it. I was stableman for one thing, and in that capacity sometimes had charge of as many as a dozen horses. Then I harnessed and 'hitched up' all the buggies and carriages, and had to keep them and the harness clean. I was milkman, milking four cows, taking charge of their calves and feeding them on hay and grass, and occasional apples and pears in the season. My spare time in the summer was devoted to picking and drying apricots, plums, greengages, magnum bonums, and peaches, and when the summer still further advanced I had to see that our fifty horses came up to water at the ranche, for the heat dried up the pools and springs in the pastures. There were 300 sheep, and these I looked after during lambing and brought to water also. Half the day I was on horseback, for the most part riding a black Californian 'broncho,' who threw me twice 'buck-jumping,' and on the first occasion nearly killed me. But before I had done with him I made him kind and tractable, teaching him some school tricks, such as backing and going sideways, and he learnt to follow me when I went on foot.

My companions were for the most part Italians, who swore most diabolical and blasphemous oaths, but who were kind and pleasant, hard workers too and steady. My particular partner was a Swede,

'Andy,' who was a sailor, and had been a passenger on the ill-fated 'Atlantic,' and he and I got along extremely well, sleeping in the same room, an apartment decorated with illustrations from the English 'Graphic' and 'Illustrated.'

I stayed there through haymaking and harvest and thrashing, until the vintage. There were 300 acres of vines—Mission, Zinfundel and Berger, and many others—for it was the largest vineyard in Sonoma Valley, and during this time I used to go down the vineyard on horseback, carrying a rifle to shoot the half-wild hogs who broke in to get the sweet, plentiful grapes. And ere the end of the vintage I left. The work was not in every way suited to me, and it grew more and more irksome as my small stock of money increased, for when I saw an avenue open for escape to England and civilisation, converse with uneducated men grew intolerable, and I longed for the society of those whose interests were not merely bucolical and pecuniary, whose talk was not of bullocks, 'for how can such get wisdom?'

So at last I bade farewell to my companions, sang 'L'Addio' to my Italian friends, and went down to San Francisco, and next day took the overland train for New York. It was a glad release for me, that swift flight overland, that triumphant progress through the long sunburnt plains of Southern California, the high plateaux of sweet-breath'd Arizona, the land of the beautiful maiden, through New Mexico of cattle and sheep and brown adobés, down the long descent of Kansas plains, through Missouri and the eastern States to the Atlantic seaboard and the roar and rush of New York City, and finally over the furrows of the ocean, blue and wonderful, the very sea that ran in ceaseless currents to the island of my birth, and England at last.

SMITH, ELDER, & CO.'S PUBLICATIONS.

PARLEYINGS WITH CERTAIN PEOPLE OF IMPORTANCE IN THEIR DAY. To wit: Bernard de Mandeville, Daniel Bartoli, Christopher Smart, George Bubb Dodington, Francis Furini, Gerard de Lairesse, and Charles Avison. Introduced by a Dialogue between Apollo and the Fates. Concluded by another between John Fust and his Friends. By ROBERT BROWNING. Fcp. 8vo. 9s.

LIFE OF HENRY FAWCETT. By LESLIE STEPHEN, Author of 'A History of English Thought in the Eighteenth Century,' 'Hours in a Library,' &c. Fourth Edition. Large crown 8vo. With 2 Steel Portraits. 12s. 6d.

A JOURNAL KEPT BY DICK DOYLE in the year 1840. Illustrated by several hundred Sketches by the Author. With an Introduction by J. HUNGERFORD POLLEN, and a Portrait. Second Edition. Demy 4to. 21s.

*** The Journal has been reproduced in facsimile, and is printed on fine paper. It is handsomely bound in cloth, and forms a very elegant gift-book.

LIFE OF FRANK BUCKLAND. By his Brother-in-Law, GEORGE C. BOMPAS, Editor of 'Notes and Jottings from Animal Life.' With a Portrait. New and Cheaper Edition. Crown 8vo. 5s.; or, gilt edges, 6s.

NOTES AND JOTTINGS FROM ANIMAL LIFE. By the late FRANK BUCKLAND. New and Cheaper Edition. With Illustrations. Crown 8vo. 5s.; or, gilt edges, 6s.

DON QUIXOTE. The Ingenious Gentleman, Don Quixote of La Mancha. By MIGUEL DE CERVANTES SAAVEDRA. A Translation, with Introduction and Notes, by JOHN ORMSBY, Translator of the 'Poem of the Cid.' 4 vols. 8vo. 12s. 6d. each.

ENGLISH LIFE IN CHINA. By Major HENRY KNOLLYS, Royal Artillery, Author of 'From Sedan to Saarbrück,' Editor of 'Incidents in the Sepoy War,' 'Incidents in the China War,' &c. Crown 8vo. 7s. 6d.

WITH HICKS PASHA IN THE SOUDAN. By Col. the Hon. J. COLBORNE, Special Correspondent of the *Daily News*. With Portrait Group of Hicks Pasha and Staff. Second Edition. Crown 8vo. 6s.

SOME LITERARY RECOLLECTIONS. By JAMES PAYN, Author of 'By Proxy' &c. Fcp. 8vo. limp cloth, 2s. 6d.

HAYTI; or, the Black Republic. By Sir SPENSER ST. JOHN, K.C.M.G., formerly Her Majesty's Minister Resident and Consul-General in Hayti, now Her Majesty's Special Envoy to Mexico. With a Map. Large crown 8vo. 7s. 6d.

THE SCOURGE OF CHRISTENDOM: Annals of British Relations with Algiers prior to the French Conquest. With Illustrations of Ancient Algiers from 1578 to 1824. By Lieutenant-Colonel R. L. PLAYFAIR, H.B.M.'s Consul to Algiers. With Illustrations. Demy 8vo. 14s.

A FALLEN IDOL. By F. ANSTEY, Author of 'Vice Versâ,' 'The Giant's Robe,' &c. Crown 8vo. 6s.

THE GIANT'S ROBE. By F. ANSTEY, Author of 'Vice Versâ.' Fourth Edition. Crown 8vo. 6s.

VICE VERSÂ; or, a Lesson to Fathers. By F. ANSTEY. Crown 8vo. 2s. 6d.

LIBERALISM IN RELIGION; and other Sermons. By W. PAGE ROBERTS, M.A., Minister of St. Peter's, Vere Street, London; formerly Vicar of Eye, Suffolk; Author of 'Law and God,' 'Reasonable Service,' &c. Second Edition. Crown 8vo. 6s.

By the same Author.

LAW AND GOD. Fifth Edition. Crown 8vo. 5s.

REASONABLE SERVICE. Fourth Edition. Crown 8vo. 6s.

London: SMITH, ELDER, & CO., 15 Waterloo Place.

SMITH, ELDER, & CO.'S PUBLICATIONS.

CITIES OF EGYPT. By REGINALD STUART POOLE. Crown 8vo. 5s.
'A book which does not contain a dull line from beginning to end.'—ACADEMY.

LEAVES FROM THE DIARY OF HENRY GREVILLE. Edited by the VISCOUNTESS ENFIELD. FIRST SERIES. 8vo. 14s. SECOND SERIES. With Portrait. 8vo. 14s.

UNDERGROUND RUSSIA: Revolutionary Profiles and Sketches from Life. By STEPNIAK, formerly Editor of 'Zemlia i Volia' (Land and Liberty). With a Preface by PETER LAVROFF. Translated from the Italian. Second Edition. Crown 8vo. 6s.

A BOOK OF SIBYLS: Mrs. Barbauld—Miss Edgeworth—Mrs. Opie—Miss Austen. By Miss THACKERAY (Mrs. Richmond Ritchie). Essays reprinted from the *Cornhill Magazine*. Large crown 8vo. 7s. 6d.

A BIRTHDAY BOOK. Designed by H.R.H. the PRINCESS BEATRICE. Printed in Colours on hand-made paper, and Illustrated by Fifteen Full-page Water-colour Drawings reproduced in the highest style of Chromo-lithography. Second Edition. 4to. 42s.

THE MATTHEW ARNOLD BIRTHDAY BOOK. Arranged by his Daughter, ELEANOR ARNOLD. Handsomely printed and bound in cloth, gilt edges. With Photograph. Small 4to. 10s. 6d.

ST. PAUL AND PROTESTANTISM; with Other Essays. Popular Edition. By MATTHEW ARNOLD. Crown 8vo. 2s. 6d.
CONTENTS:—St. Paul and Protestantism—Puritanism and the Church of England—Modern Dissent—A Comment on Christmas.

MORE LEAVES FROM THE JOURNAL OF A LIFE IN THE HIGHLANDS, from 1862 to 1882. Fifth Edition, with Portraits and Woodcut Illustrations, 8vo. 10s. 6d.
*** Also the Popular Edition, with Portrait and Woodcut Illustrations. Fcp. 8vo. 2s. 6d.

SIX MONTHS IN THE RANKS; or, the Gentleman Private. Crown 8vo. 2s. 6d.

EXTRACTS FROM THE WRITINGS OF W. M. THACKERAY, Chiefly Philosophical and Reflective. Cheap Edition. Fcp. 8vo. 2s. 6d.

TANTLER'S SISTER, AND OTHER UNTRUTHFUL STORIES; being a Collection of Pieces Written for Public Reading. By EDWARD F. TURNER, Author of 'T Leaves.' Third Edition. Crown 8vo. 3s. 6d.

T LEAVES: a Collection of Pieces for Public Reading. By EDWARD F. TURNER, Author of 'Tantler's Sister' &c. Third Edition. Crown 8vo. 3s. 6d.

THE LIFE OF HIS ROYAL HIGHNESS THE PRINCE CONSORT. By Sir THEODORE MARTIN, K.C.B. With Portrait and Views. 5 vols. Demy 8vo. 18s. each.
*** Also a 'People's Edition,' in 1 vol., bound in cloth, 4s. 6d.; or in six parts, price 6d. each. Cloth Cases for binding, 1s. each.

SHAKESPEARE. Certain Selected Plays Abridged for the Use of the Young. By SAMUEL BRANDRAM, M.A. Oxon. Third Edition. Large Crown 8vo. 6s.
*** Also separately, in 9 Parts, cloth limp, 6d. each.

SHAKSPEARE'S KNOWLEDGE AND USE OF THE BIBLE. By CHARLES WORDSWORTH, D.C.L., Bishop of S. Andrews, and Fellow of Winchester College. Third Edition. With Appendix containing additional Illustrations and Tercentenary Sermon preached at Stratford-on-Avon. Crown 8vo. 7s. 6d.
*** Also bound in calf, 12s.; or, in morocco, gilt edges, 16s.

SHAKSPEARE COMMENTARIES. By Dr. G. G. GERVINUS, Professor at Heidelberg. Translated, under the Author's superintendence, by F. E. BUNNETT. With a Preface by F. J. FURNIVALL, Esq. New Edition, revised. 8vo. 14s.

London: SMITH, ELDER, & CO., 15 Waterloo Place.

SMITH, ELDER, & CO.'S PUBLICATIONS.

THE LIFE OF LORD LAWRENCE. By R. BOSWORTH SMITH, M.A., late Fellow of Trinity College, Oxford; Assistant Master at Harrow School; Author of 'Mohammed and Mohammedanism,' 'Carthage and the Carthaginians,' &c. New, Revised, and Cheaper Edition, being the Sixth Edition. 2 vols. large crown 8vo. with 2 Portraits and 2 Maps, 21s.

LIFE OF SIR HENRY LAWRENCE. By Major-General Sir HERBERT BENJAMIN EDWARDES, K.C.B., K.C.S.I., and HERMAN MERIVALE, C.B. With Two Portraits. 8vo. 12s.

LIFE OF LIEUT.-GENERAL SIR JAMES OUTRAM. By Major-General Sir FREDERIC J. GOLDSMID, C.B., K.C.S.I. Second Edition. 2 vols. demy 8vo. 32s.

MOHAMMED AND MOHAMMEDANISM: Lectures delivered at the Royal Institution of Great Britain in February and March 1874. By R. BOSWORTH SMITH, M.A. Second Edition, Revised, with considerable Additions. Crown 8vo. 8s. 6d.

THE MERV OASIS: Travels and Adventures East of the Caspian during the Years 1879-80-81, including Five Months' Residence among the Tekkes of Merv. By EDMOND O'DONOVAN, Special Correspondent of the *Daily News*. In 2 vols. demy 8vo., with Portrait, Maps, and Facsimiles of State Documents, 36s.

MERV: a Story of Adventures and Captivity. Epitomised from 'The Merv Oasis.' By EDMOND O'DONOVAN, Special Correspondent of the *Daily News*. With a Portrait. Crown 8vo. 6s.

WALKS IN FLORENCE AND ITS ENVIRONS. By SUSAN and JOANNA HORNER. New Edition, Revised and Enlarged, with numerous Illustrations. 2 vols. crown 8vo. 21s.

THE LIFE OF MAHOMET. With Introductory Chapters on the Original Sources for the Biography of Mahomet, and on the Pre-Islamite History of Arabia. By Sir WILLIAM MUIR, LL.D. 4 vols. demy 8vo. 32s.

THE LIFE OF MAHOMET. From Original Sources. By Sir WILLIAM MUIR, LL.D. A New and Cheaper Edition, in one volume. With Maps. 8vo. 14s.

ANNALS OF THE EARLY CALIPHATE. By Sir WILLIAM MUIR, K.C.S.I., Author of 'The Life of Mahomet,' &c. With Map. 8vo. 16s.

ESSAYS ON THE EXTERNAL POLICY OF INDIA. By the late J. W. S. WYLLIE, C.S.I., India Civil Service, sometime Acting Foreign Secretary to the Government of India. Edited, with a brief Life, by W. W. HUNTER, B.A., LL.D. With a Portrait of the Author. 8vo. 14s.

EGYPT OF THE PHARAOHS AND OF THE KHEDIVE. By the Rev. F. BARHAM ZINCKE. Second Edition. Demy 8vo. 16s.

THE ANNALS OF RURAL BENGAL. From Official Records and the Archives of Ancient Families. By W. W. HUNTER, LL.D. Vol. I. The Ethnical Frontier. Fifth Edition. Demy 8vo. 18s.

By the same Author.

ORISSA; or, The Vicissitudes of an Indian Province under Native and British Rule. Being the Second and Third Volumes of 'Annals of Rural Bengal.' With Illustrations. 2 vols. demy 8vo. 32s.

A LIFE OF THE EARL OF MAYO, Fourth Viceroy of India. 2 vols. Second Edition. Demy 8vo. 24s.

London: SMITH, ELDER, & CO., 15 Waterloo Place.

SMITH, ELDER, & CO.'S PUBLICATIONS.

MEMOIRS OF LIFE AND WORK. By CHARLES J. B. WILLIAMS, M.D., F.R.S., Physician Extraordinary to Her Majesty the Queen. With a Portrait of the Author, and Original Sketches of La Place, Laennec, Andral, and other French *savants*. 8vo. 16s.

MEMORIES OF OLD FRIENDS. Being Extracts from the Journals and Letters of Caroline Fox, of Penjerrick, Cornwall, from 1835 to 1871, to which are added Fourteen Original Letters from J. S. Mill, never before published. Edited by HORACE N. PYM. Fourth Edition. With a Portrait. 2 vols. crown 8vo. 18s.

* *New and Revised Edition in One Volume. With Portrait. Crown 8vo. 7s. 6d.*

THE LAW RELATING TO TRADE MARKS. By R. S. MUSHET, of Lincoln's Inn, Barrister-at-Law. Crown 8vo. 5s.

THE FIRST BOOK OF EUCLID MADE EASY FOR BEGINNERS. Arranged from 'The Elements of Euclid' by ROBERT SIMSON, M.D. By WILLIAM HOWARD. With Unlettered Diagrams with Coloured Lines. Crown 8vo. 5s.

PATCHWORK. By FREDERICK LOCKER. Small crown 8vo. 5s.

ESSAYS ON ART. By J. COMYNS CARR. Crown 8vo. 7s. 6d.

HISTORY OF ART. By Dr. WILHELM LÜBKE. Translated by F. E. BUNNETT. With 415 Illustrations. Third Edition. 2 vols. Imp. 8vo. 42s.

HISTORY OF SCULPTURE FROM THE EARLIEST PERIOD TO THE PRESENT TIME. Translated by F. E. BUNNETT. A New Edition. 377 Illustrations. 2 vols. Imp. 8vo. 42s.

STRAY PAPERS. By JOHN ORMSBY, Author of 'Autumn Rambles in North Africa.' Crown 8vo. 7s. 6d.

THE LIFE AND LETTERS OF SYDNEY DOBELL. Edited by F. J. With Steel Portrait and Photographic Illustrations. 2 vols. Crown 8vo. 28s.

FRENCH PICTURES IN ENGLISH CHALK. By the Author of 'The Member for Paris,' &c. &c. First Series. Crown 8vo. 7s. 6d. Second Series. Crown 8vo. 7s. 6d.

GEOLOGICAL OBSERVATIONS ON THE VOLCANIC ISLANDS and PARTS of SOUTH AMERICA visited during the Voyage of H.M.S. *Beagle*. By CHARLES DARWIN, M.A., F.R.S., Author of 'The Origin of Species,' &c. A New Edition, with Maps and Illustrations. Crown 8vo. 12s. 6d.

THE POWER OF SOUND. By EDMUND GURNEY, late Fellow of Trinity College, Cambridge. Royal 8vo. 25s.

THE AUTOBIOGRAPHY OF HARRIET MARTINEAU. With Memorials by MARIA WESTON CHAPMAN. With Portraits and Views. Third Edition. 3 vols. 32s.

FARMING IN A SMALL WAY. By JAMES LONG, Author of 'Poultry for Prizes and Profit,' 'The Goat,' &c. Crown 8vo. 7s. 6d.

PRINCIPLES OF REFORM, POLITICAL AND LEGAL. By JOHN BOYD KINNEAR. Demy 8vo. 7s. 6d.

By the same Author.

PRINCIPLES OF PROPERTY IN LAND. Crown 8vo. 5s.

London: SMITH, ELDER, & CO., 15 Waterloo Place.

www.ingramcontent.com/pod-product-compliance
Lightning Source LLC
Chambersburg PA
CBHW030018240426
43672CB00007B/1004